A New Missionary Era

A New Missionary Era

EDITED BY
PADRAIG FLANAGAN, S.P.S.

ORBIS BOOKS
Maryknoll, New York 10545

The Catholic Foreign Mission Society of America (Maryknoll) recruits and trains people for overseas missionary service. Through Orbis Books Maryknoll aims to foster the international dialogue that is essential to mission. The books published, however, reflect the opinions of their authors and are not meant to represent the offical position of the society.

Library of Congress Cataloging in Publication Data

Main entry under title:

A New missionary era.

    1. Missions—Addresses, essays, lectures.
1. Flanagan, Padraig.
BV2070.N48   266'.2'0904   81-9595
ISBN 0-88344-331-7 (pbk.)   AACR2

CONTENTS

v

PART FOUR
THE CHALLENGE OF JUSTICE

PART FIVE
MAKING THE CHURCH INCARNATE

PREFACE

The title *A New Missionary Era* may be intriguing to some readers. Does it imply that an "old" missionary era is over and a "new" one has begun? Does it contrast the two eras and does it support one over the other?

The new missionary era was officially ushered into the Roman Catholic church by the documents of Vatican II; it was strengthened by subsequent documents of Rome and of other local churches and it finds its solid ground and some of its major trends in them. The document on the *Church's Missionary Activity* (*Ad Gentes*) grounded mission at the very heart of the church and stressed the recognition of the local churches throughout the world. *The Dogmatic Constitution on the Church* (*Lumen Gentium*) offered us the image of the Church as "People of God" more than institution—people alive in the Word and in the Spirit and thus missionary people. Its twin decree on the *Pastoral Constitution on the Church in the Modern World* (*Gaudium et Spes*) stressed the centrality of the kingdom to mission and proclaimed that all human beings "by their labor are unfolding the Creator's work" and are contributing to "the realization in history of the divine plan," thus broadening the concept of mission and the areas of missionary activity.

The Synod of Bishops contributed new dimensions and orientations to the church's mission. *Justice in the World* (1971) declared that the doing of justice is a "constitutive dimension of the preaching of the Gospel." *Evangelization in the Modern World* (1974) dealt with the whole question of cultures and mission.

The documents of Medellín (1968) and of Puebla (1979) asked that the Latin American church opt for the poor by becoming poor itself and by learning from the poor the modern understanding of the Gospel; it also proposed basic, or grassroots, Christian communities as a model of Christian community valid for our times.

A document of the Asian Bishops (1974) strongly recommended that the church in mission be in dialogue with the ancient religions and cultures not only to make Christianity more acceptable, but to continue the process of incarnation begun by the Word. Theologians, missionaries, and grassroots people who, prior to the publication of the above documents had talked about these aspects of mission in a timid way, were encouraged by the same documents and began to study these new trends more deeply, to reflect on them more thoroughly, and to share them more boldly. Missionaries especially began to take very seriously, not only the documents of the church, but also their own experiences. They began to look at their sending churches and found that there was great apathy, that they had lost the sense of mission, and that they, too, were in need of mission from other churches. They looked at the churches of their service and discovered new life, beautiful values, a different way of being church, religious, community. And they coined the term "Mutuality of Mission," which denotes a new trend and which demands that the missioners who have experienced other ways of being Christians have a responsibility to enrich the life and activities of the sending churches.

The missioners also looked at their countries of origin, at the policies of their governments and the activities of the transnationals, and they found that in many instances these factors were the major cause of the poverty missioners were trying to eradicate and of the oppression they were trying to eliminate. And so the missioners discovered another aspect of mission, i.e., to correct in their own countries the causes of poverty and injustice of so many people in the world. They coined another term, "Reverse Mission," to connote this particular aspect of mission.

The missioners became clearly aware that with their own activities—which in the words of *Evangelii Nuntiandi* were meant to share the "Good News with the whole of creation so that creation may be renewed from within"—they in fact exported a Western awareness of that "Good News" and transplanted a Western church which then imposed itself on all the other people with consequences that threaten the very life of the Gospel and the existence of the church itself. They took seriously the invitation of Vatican II and of the Synod on Evangelization to incarnate the Gospel and the church in the cultures of people so that, as Pope John Paul II said to the bishops of Kenya, "Christ himself would be African."

The work of inculturation can be seriously undertaken only if people are free to approach the Gospel, to reflect on it in the situations in which they live, and to respond to the demands of the Gospel in their lives. This cannot be done in ordinary congregations. It is possible only in small faith communities where there is freedom of expression, where all are heard, and where all are important agents of the kingdom. And the local churches, with the missioners, established "Comunidades Eclesiales de Base," or "Small Faith Communities."

These small communities very soon began to have their own leaders, to demand new leaders, to question the present system of ministry in the church. And the movement for other ministries, new ministries, new ways of sharing the regular ministries in the church began. This movement has so far produced only a few fruits, but it promises more and different fruits in the future.

Once these and other new elements of the church's mission in the modern world had been reflected upon and had become new orientations in the praxis of mission, the need to share them with all the segments (audiences) of the church was felt by the missioners. Partial attempts were made through the help of national mission councils, pontifical mission agencies, missionary congregations, and some centers of higher learning to provide moments of reflection and of sharing among interested people. But what about the entire church? Would it be possible to share these new elements of mission with all the people of the church?

A very comprehensive attempt at doing such reflection by a whole church was attempted at a National Missionary Congress held at the Shrine of Knock, Ireland, in April 1979. Representatives of the whole Irish church convened at Knock during the ten-day Congress organized by the Irish Missionary Union in cooperation with the Irish Missionary Council and the Pontifical Missionary Agencies. The Missionary Congress prepared a special (core) program for missioners and people involved in the cross-cultural mission of the Irish church. This program was offered primarily in the mornings and evenings of the Congress. Concomitantly, during the late morning and early afternoon hours of each day, various groups of people came to the Shrine to participate for a few hours in special daily programs geared to the groups themselves.

This book contains most of the major presentations delivered at the Missionary Congress by many prominent speakers from all over the world. With an easy and popular style, the speakers touch upon most of the elements which make for a new missionary era. Rightly, the book opens with an overview of mission and its major challenges, plus a brief description of mission as perceived by the people of the "mission" continents. Since mission is to, in, for, and with the world, then it is very important to understand the world's situations in order to exercise a meaningful mission.

Several aspects of this new missionary era are contemplated in the second part of the book, and a mention is made of important characteristics for the missioner and for the church. The last two parts of the book develop what might be considered the most urgent aspects of mission: the need for inculturation and the necessity to include justice in all aspects of mission. Thus, this book reflects the major elements of mission as expressed by Vatican II and subsequent church teaching and documents, and it furthers them in the light of new and recent developments, of new insights of missioners, of new awareness of people and the lived experience of the speakers themselves and of the participants.

I was one of those participants, and as I read this book, I re-lived the beautiful experience of the Irish Missionary Congress. I am hoping that all those who will read it, but did not participate in the Missionary Congress will, nevertheless, capture all its deep meaning and at least some of the thrill and enthusiasm for this new missionary era which was evident at the Missionary Congress of Knock.

Anthony Bellagamba, I.M.C.
Executive Secretary,
U.S. Catholic Mission Council

PART ONE:
MISSION IN
THE WORLD TODAY

1

CONVERSION AND MISSION

Enda McDonagh

In 1968 at the Mission Conference in Dalgan I was asked to give the opening talk, so it may be useful to look back at what we had hoped for in 1968 and see where we are now. This is not in any sense of recrimination or repentance. It is simply to glance briefly at the themes that emerged there. The book that came from that congress was entitled "The Church's Mission," with the emphasis on every member of the church being a missionary. That was in the heady days after Vatican II when we were thinking of the New Pentecost and the church becoming missionary in the full sense, in everybody. Perhaps a little later and wiser we might think that what is everybody's business might turn out to be nobody's business. Not that we suggested dismantling the mission societies or replacing them in any way, but we did look to a renewal of the church in a missionary sense that would make it a genuinely "missionary people."

A second theme that certainly surfaced was an emphasis on mission as the interchange between equals: that, in fact, we were not going from Europe to Asia or Africa either as imperialists or simply paternalists, giving them what we had got, so to speak. We were there to receive as well as to give. There was a second aspect to that mission of interchange which seemed to us important at the time—that the church in Ireland which had given a great deal of remarkable people to the missionary countries should in turn be receiving back into its own personnel, into its own ideas, into its own apostolic activity and prayer life some return from the missionary countries; that it should be open to that return, that it should be expecting and integrating that return.

A further element that was clearly in our minds at the time was that a church that is alive, a church that is incarnated in a particular culture, is a church that is a reflecting church, a church that is developing the faith. We spoke of the signs of a native theology as indicating the depth and vitality, that is, the witness of the church. I think we can say very fairly that the remarkable development in indigenous theology in those areas which we thought of as mission countries at that time has been truly God-given. So I

Fr. Enda McDonagh is professor of moral theology at St. Patrick's College, Maynooth—on leave of absence to the University of Notre Dame, Indiana.

3

would venture to say that the vital theology that one reads of today tends to come from Africa and Asia and Latin America rather than from the more sedate and perhaps tired churches of Europe and North America.

Another more practical idea that was discussed at the time and which surfaces in questions today was the whole question of missionary training and the missionary dimension of all priestly and religious training, the need for research into mission projects, the need for a mission institute. Something of that has come and something has not. Some progress can be reported.

That was 1968. Where would a missionary people stand today? Let us look at the mission and missionary rather than the people. Around the word "mission" a whole cluster of ideas or related words can be found. We think of the missionary as somebody sent to preach the Gospel, an apostle in that older sense, to preach the Gospel so that people may be converted, echoing the message of Jesus and his apostles, "Do penance, be converted, for the kingdom is at hand." Another version of the same idea is implanting or building the church. We could pursue many of these ideas. I wish to pursue one because I think it illumines the others in a certain way, but there is nothing special about it; it is in no way superior to the others. I wish to take the idea of "conversion."

In some ways conversion is having a bad press. We think that the ecumenical movement means that people do not need to be converted. The positive attitude we have developed towards other religions and, indeed, to all people of good will and the universal saving power of God seems to have taken the bite out of conversion.

If we adopt the other word, "repentance," we find it is not doing so well either, especially if we are to judge by the criticisms we hear about the decline in the practice of confession or about the need to present Christianity as a joyous Easter reality and get away from the pessimism of sin. So, it might do no harm to have a look at conversion because whether we think of the sixth, seventh or eighth centuries or of the nineteenth and twentieth centuries, we think of missionaries going out to convert.

That notion of conversion was, perhaps, too simple, but the simplification had a point. We were preaching the Gospel so that people might hear and be converted and believe and have the fullness of the life of Christ. We were naive and innocent sometimes, but it was a naiveté and innocence both of faith in the power of God who gave the harvest and a naiveté and innocence of concern for these people. But it was a naiveté and innocence that, at the same time, could not distinguish the faith from the baggage with it, could not see past the souls to be saved to the people who were in pain, the people who were exploited and who had myriad other needs. Of course, in education and in medicine we did heroic work in attending to those in need, but somehow we thought of it as a work of charity, not really missionary work. Nowadays, and departing from Paul VI's use of the term, we speak of evangelization more as a dialogue and think in terms of our relationship with the other churches, with other religions and, indeed, with all people. We are more sensitive to where they are rather than where we simply want them to be. More sensitive to them in their particularity, their cultural particularity as Africans or Asians, their religious particularities, members of African traditional religions, Hinduism, Mohammedanism, or whatever. What is happening, I would suggest, is that in a very basic and a very true sense, we are being converted to them, and this, I believe, is at the heart of our missionary work.

I think that always when we heard the call, when we saw ourselves as sent to preach the Gospel, there was a basic turning to the people, the people of Africa or Asia. But now, perhaps, we see more of the depth of that conversion. We see that if we would share with them this faith in Christ, we have to share it sensitively and delicately, not trampling over them, not being the fighting elephants who hurt the grass, but entering into their world, listening to their view of reality, not as a kind of missionary tactic or pastoral trick, but because we know now that the God whom we worship is already at work there, that the God of Jesus Christ has a million faces and these faces are black and brown and yellow and that what we are endeavoring to do is, by being converted to them and by sharing their world, enabling them to share ours. By being with them and listening to them we begin to decipher the visage of God in their belief, in their personal lives, in their love, in their community structure, so that we are not trapped in the simple cultural expression of our own belief. There is no belief that is not culturally expressed. We cannot say, "I believe in God," without using language, and language is the most concrete expression of our culture. So, we have to enter into their language, their world, the moving of the spirit within them. Being converted in this way to their particularity, their social and historical particularity, is slow and difficult and risky; the turning to God in them is the establishment of a faith community with them. As we turn to them we hope they turn to us. But we entrust ourselves out of the God who is in us to the God who is in them, that the meeting between us may be transforming, converting, for both of us, that we may grow up into the knowledge and the love of Christ.

There are some other ways of putting this. What we are doing in a sense, in turning to these people, is offering ourselves to them rather than offering simply a doctrine to them. We offer ourselves to them as embodied believers; to people who are also in some sense under the call of God, however it may be expressed or understood by them. What we are offering them is, in another fashion, the fullness of life, the fullness of themselves. What we are doing in missionary work is letting them be themselves. We are not trying to catch them for our club. We are not trying to make them statistics on our registers. What we are trying to do is to establish community with them which we know to be community based on our shared sisterhood and brotherhood of Christ, our shared daughterhood and sonship with the Father. Because, as they grow and become themselves, they become more fully brothers and sisters of Christ, daughters and sons of the Father. That sharing of ourselves, and of the Gospel, makes enormous demands because we are not just Gospel people, we are a mixture of belief and unbelief. All we can pray is that we believe and ask help for our unbelief—that our unbelief might connect with their unbelief, might reinforce their unbelief. On the other hand, their very difference, their very otherness in their awareness of humanity and the mystery of humanity and its final mystery in God, is at least a corrective for us. It opens up our vision of God so that it is not so narrow and restricted, but the God of Jesus Christ is seen as the God of all cultures and all peoples, as the God who is at the heart of every person.

It is not easy; it takes time and patience. Perhaps we are coming to a stage where the missionary people will have to have much more patience and much more time. We will have to sow the seed and let the harvest come when it will, unlike the worldly value of quick results. A profit balance cannot be so easily counted. In fact, the faith that is in us may not see such quick and easy return. The return may be in hope only, because we have to allow for the time of growth, a time that is hidden in God himself.

The risks are many. Let us just look at some of the communities to which we may be summoned in the power of the gospel, to which we may and should be converted. For example, we talk a great deal about the church of the poor, our solidarity with the poor, the difficulty of reconciling the God of the poor with the God of the rich, the difficulty of how Dives and Lazarus can have the same vision of God.

In a way our conversion to the poor is the most obvious necessity, perhaps the easiest to defend theoretically and the hardest to carry out in practice. Yet if we are not prepared to share slums and shantytowns, if the missionary people can no longer send forth from itself people who will take on the perspective of the poor by entering into their lives, by waiting to learn from them where they might discern God, where the Kingdom might come from, where the development into the fullness of Christ might emerge, the missionary people has lost its vitality. And, of course, this sharing of poverty means sharing the frustration, the limitation, the oppression. It means sharing the sin of humankind bearing on these people and it sees the call to change that situation, the social structure in which these people are caught. It sees, as the Latin Americans see, that the conversion we are looking for is a conversion of people but also a conversion of structures. This conversion of structures is not only that the poor may grow up into the fullness of Christ, but that the rich, the oppressors, and the indifferent may be freed from their false gods and their own enslaving chains.

We could look at it in terms of race and see the same kind of thing, or we could look at it in terms of poverty and race as they coincide so frequently around the world. We could look at it in terms of sex and see how far the oppression of women is a distortion of God and how far our male-dominated church is unable to present the full image of God. We could look at it as I did so painfully in South Africa, and see how poverty and race and sex are pinned together to give one of the most violently blasphemous expressions of humanity's inhumanity.

We can experience the need to do this but we are good at finding excuses.

Why us? I, in particular, should not do it! When it comes to entering into the cultural world of the other it is even more difficult. One cannot simply shed one's European heritage. One can never become simply an African or an Asian. It is not easy for us to enter into the other culture, and yet I think that the sharing, the conversion to the culture of the others, is enormously enriching for us as well as releasing for us; and it is enriching for them. We might too easily take the line that, because in the past we brutally thrust into others' cultural forms, we should now simply withdraw. For one thing it is too late to do so in many places; and for another thing, a culture that is turned in on itself does not develop. So they have need of the West, but not always the kind of need we filled in the past.

In our missionary conversion role we have not only to take account of cultural differences in this fashion, to be converted to them and by them. We have to take account of religious differences, and this is the most difficult thing of all. It is the area that people find most difficult, because it seems to somehow betray the truth of our own community, our own religion. Can Christians genuinely enter into the tradition of the Hindu without somehow sacrificing their Christianity? I think the truth is we don't know. But there are people who are exploring this, and they need patience and time. I think it is the way that we have to go with many of these advanced religions. Our conversion in some way has to be to the Hindus, if they would be opened to Christ explicitly. And as we are converted to the Hindus we cannot entirely avoid their Hinduism. It is a part of them which is critical to them. This is an area in which we feel hesitant, in which the risks seem great. It is the area in which charges of indifference or betrayal can be so easily hurled around, and yet the fact that the God who is so different from humankind could empty himself to the point of entering into humanity is a kind of parable for us here. But what criteria do we set up? How do we go about it? Is it some kind of joint Hindu-Christian community, as already exists in some places? How far are we drawn into the Hindu way? Whatever the Hindus may think about it, we have the responsibility to make the move. We are the people who know about Jesus Christ, who believe that he is also at the heart of the Hindu's salvation. We have to try to share in their world, at their level, that it may be opened up to that fulfillment in Christ.

Nearer home there is the question of our relationships with the other churches. The conversion rate, it has been said, has been ruined by ecumenism. But is that the deepest meaning of conversion, that we can count them on our register rather than on theirs?

Conversion to the others—where they are, as what they are, as in themselves embodying Jesus Christ, as in themselves daughters and sons of the Father, as in themselves enriching for us and opening us up to fuller understanding and commitment to God—that is part of the missionary vocation today.

In that kind of mission, in that kind of conversion—which I think is in basic continuity with what we knew in the past, although there are clear developments—we are letting the people be more fully themselves. That is in a sense what Pope John Paul is talking about when he speaks of Christ the Redeemer in his recent encyclical: the full and true humanity, the old phrase about "the fullness of man is the glory of God." Letting, enabling, helping them to be themselves, from the very heart of their relationship with God and with one another, draws us into the kind of religious social transformation we have been talking about. We can stand back from that, or kneel back from it and get on our knees and attempt our daily prayer and think in catechism terms that the prayer is raising our hearts and minds to God, that it is, as we say, letting God be present to us in our lives. But what our mission activity is all about is letting God be more fully present to all people. Letting him be more fully himself, in his images, his daughters and his sons.

It seems to me that the thrust of that is both exhilarating and frightening. That is what the God of Jesus Christ has entrusted to us: that we would let him be himself in his own world. That is, that Christ is not primarily about the liberation of human beings, but the liberation of God.

This means setting God free to be himself in the minds and hearts, the structures, the cultures, the languages, aspirations, frustrations, the fulfillment of all people. So, whether we pray or whether we missionize, and whether we missionize in purely religious terms or in caring and aiding terms, what we are doing in allowing and enabling people to be more fully themselves is setting God free, letting him enter his own world, enjoy his own world as himself.

It may have been some sense of that which inspired one woman to say, "My soul magnifies the Lord and my spirit rejoices in God my Savior." God sought the consent of that simple peasant woman that he might be himself, fully himself, in human form in Jesus Christ. He is now asking our consent that he might be more fully himself in all humankind.

2

NEW CHALLENGES—NEW HOPES

Donal Dorr

I propose to give an outline of six major challenges facing the missionary Church today. But in order to do this in a meaningful way I need first to sketch the background against which these challenges arise. So the first part of this paper looks at the background, under the following headings: economic, political, social, cultural, religious, ecclesiastical.

BACKGROUND

Economic Background

If I were asked to identify what is specific to missionary work I would say that it is working in a cross-cultural situation, not just crossing any cultural barrier but working to enable Christianity to take root in cultures where it has not yet become embedded. But it happens that in most cases the cross-cultural barrier coincides with the barrier between the rich countries and the poor ones. Apart from the outstanding exception of Japan, most of the areas where missionaries work belong to the Third World, the poor world. Later I shall be noting that this situation poses a great challenge to the missionary church. But at this point I simply want to indicate briefly what kind of situation we are dealing with. It is not merely that these countries are desperately poor, with an average income in some cases of one-fiftieth of our average income. Such poverty was not quite so shocking so long as there was a reasonable hope that it could be overcome. But the past five or six years have shown that this is highly unlikely. The energy crisis (and a series of related problems such as shortages of fertilizers and other basic materials) has undermined whatever hope the poor countries had of escaping quickly from the poverty trap. But, more importantly, it has shown how weak and vulnerable the economies of the poor countries are—and how they come off second-best when they have to compete with the rich countries for scarce resources.

Fr. Donal Dorr is a member of St. Patrick's Missionary Society at present engaged in research into the theology of development at St. Patrick's College, Maynooth.

The greatest economic problem of most of the poor countries is their *dependence*. They may have gained nominal political independence. But in fact they are not independent in any very meaningful sense because the terms of their trade with the wealthy countries are so unfavorable; they are not in a position to drive a good bargain and this weakness leads to others, especially the need to get foreign aid (with strings attached) and to borrow money (also with many strings attached).

Political Background

Economic difficulties give rise to political problems. It is not surprising to find that many of the poor countries of the world suffer from great political instability. This in turn gives rise to a good deal of repression. But there is also another reason for repression, one that is even more directly related to economics. In practice this nearly always means widening the gap within a country between the rich and the poor. It means creating a privileged "elite" that benefits from the new agricultural and industrial and commercial growth. The theory is that much of the new wealth will trickle down to the poor. But in practice the poor are often more exploited than ever. So an elaborate and repressive security system develops to protect the privileged group. Opposition is driven underground and the only likelihood of effective change is through violent revolution.

Social Changes

Most of the poor countries of the world are undergoing tremendous social upheaval. The traditional patterns of life are changing or breaking down very rapidly indeed. This is associated particularly with a very rapid growth of the urban areas. The towns and cities have acted as magnets drawing in the people from the rural areas; and in the process the traditional fabric of life and behavior has broken down to a very considerable extent. People believe that in the towns and cities they can find the opportunity to live the Western life-style, so they are drawn to the urban areas. They have continued to pour into the cities even though there is very little hope for most of those who now come into them. There is not only a *pull* to the urban areas but also a *push* from the rural areas. This is due partly to the great increase in the population. But another cause is a change in the style of agriculture. The traditional type of farming was to grow food for the local people. The new type of farming puts a lot of emphasis on "cash crops" which are to be sold on the world market. Obviously if a lot of the land is being used to support cash crops then there will not be as much food at home to support people who live on the land.

Cultural Difficulties

Alongside the great social changes in most poor countries today we note that a tremendous cultural invasion is taking place. Traditional values and outlooks are giving way to the Western approach. There is a wide generation gap between parents who have been educated in the traditional tribal manner and their children who attend schools committed to giving them a Western type of education. There is very little that the two approaches to life have in common. Parents have largely abdicated all right to tell their children how they ought to live or what the meaning of life really is. The new generation live in great uncertainty. Many of them have a love-hate attitude to their own values and culture. Let me explain what I mean by referring to my own experience. When people of my generation were growing up in the west of Ireland we felt ashamed of traditional Irish values and ways of doing things. We were embarrassed about our accent and our customs. But at the same time we also resented people who spoke with an English accent. So at the same time we had attitudes of love and of hate for our own culture. This kind of phenomenon is common in the Third World today. Of course, it is much more serious there because the clash is not just between two very similar cultures (the Irish and the English) but between totally different outlooks, that of the West and the traditional ways of Africa and Asia.

Religious Background

When I look at the Third World from a religious point of view what impresses me most of all is that, in spite of the tremendous economic difficulties, the political instability, the social upheaval, and the cultural invasion, there still remains a deep religious sense in most of the poorer countries of the world. In Africa, for instance, one might have expected that the growth of the cities and the increasing dominance of Western values would have led to the abandonment of religion. In one sense this is true insofar as religion took the form of traditional local cults. Very many of those who come to the cities have had some Western schooling; and this means in practice that they have already abandoned traditional religious practices to a considerable extent. Migration to the city reinforces this. Obviously, if people have been used to worshipping in a certain forest or at a certain river, then when they go to the city they can no longer perform those particular religious rites. But in spite of this, the people who come to the cities do not lose their religious sense. They may have to give up their traditional religious practices, but at least some of the traditional attitudes may find alternative forms of expression. Perhaps one reason for the very rapid growth of the pentecostal-type praying-and-healing churches is that they are much closer than the mainline churches to the traditional forms of religion. People who are more "respectable," more Westernized, and more "successful" tend to turn more to the mainline churches.

Ecclesiastical Background

We can now go on to look briefly at the ecclesiastical background without making the assumption that it is just the same as the religious background.

Success or failure of the church is not a sufficient measure of the strength or weakness of religion in the area.

In the past two generations the church in Africa has been going through one of the most rapid expansions that has ever occurred in history. This suggests that Christianity is able to provide for African people an articulation and expression that meets many of their religious needs. (But we should not ignore the fact that Islam is also expanding rapidly and it too strikes deep chords in many African hearts.)

In Asia the missionary situation is very different. Apart from the Philippines (which has a pattern rather similar to that of Latin America) Christians remain a small minority in Asia. Does this mean that the church has failed? It may indicate some failures on the part of the church. But I think we should also try to understand this from a sociological point of view. In the Asian situation the church is face to face with major world religions and not just with traditional religions as it was (and is) in parts of Africa where it has expanded so rapidly. The world religions have already learned to cope with the problem of transfer of their adherents from one place to another and even from a rural background to an urban background. When Muslim or Hindu people move from the country into a city like Calcutta they do not have to abandon the religious practices in which they grew up. In the non-Islamic parts of Africa, on the other hand, it may seem to many people that only by converting to Christianity can they be both modern and religious. This difference is very significant for an understanding of the success or failure of Christian missionary activity.

Although the number of Christians in Asia remains relatively tiny, nevertheless we should note that Christianity has had an enormous effect on the cultures and religions of Asia. Its beliefs and values (for instance its social and political teachings) have had a considerable influence, far beyond its own membership. So we should not be too disheartened by the fact that the number of Christians in Asia is still a tiny proportion of the total population.

In Latin America the church's understanding of its position and mission has changed radically in the past fifteen years. The documents of Medellín and Puebla give expression to the change. But equally significant is what is happening on the ground. Here I wish merely to refer to a point which might be overlooked. In accepting its prophetic role in many (but not all) areas of Latin America, the church is also accepting that it may no longer be the church of the masses. Much stricter policies about who is admitted to baptism may well lead to a situation where only a relatively small proportion of the population will be members of the church. On the other hand recent emphasis on popular religion may help to correct the trend towards a church that consists only of a small, deeply-committed group of activists. The tension between the two approaches is a healthy one; and the church on other continents has much to learn from the Latin American church's efforts to work out a balance.

In Latin America, social and political issues play a dominant role in the life of the church; and this is also the case to an increasing extent in the Caribbean. In Asia and Africa these questions are also coming to the fore; but here the cultural question seems to be even more basic. How can the church be authentically Indian, Japanese, African? About three hundred years ago in India and China some pioneer attempts were made to answer this kind of question. But these were quickly stifled and the missionary church remained basically Western in outlook. Now at last the question is being raised again—and in a context where we can hope for satisfactory answers. For, despite the enormous cultural impact the West is having on other cultures, the myth of Western cultural superiority is being challenged—not least in the places where future church leaders arc being educated. The problems of inculturation now facing the church are perhaps as radical as those which faced St. Paul when he sought to disentangle the Christian faith from its Jewish garb. It is an exciting time to be a Christian, and, above all, to be a missionary.

SIX MAJOR CHALLENGES

The Social Challenge

Having looked briefly at the background we can now consider the major challenges facing the missionary church today. The first of these is the social challenge. The question is whether the church can be a church for the poor, a church that seeks justice for those who are oppressed, a church that gives people a sense of their own dignity, a church that works for human rights at all levels. Within the past decade there has been a remarkable growth in the church's consciousness of its call to work for justice. This is true both of the Catholic church and of the major Protestant churches. There is very little room for doubt about the official church teaching on the issue of justice. The Synod of 1971 and a succession of very strong papal statements have made the church's position very clear. However the response of the church at the local level has varied very considerably. Latin America has shown the way in the past decade. There, in most of the countries at least, the church has taken a decisive "option for the poor." It is no longer simply a church *of* the poor but a church which works on behalf of those who are on the margin of society and seeks to give them a sense of their God-given dignity and rights.

The social challenge facing the church must not be limited to the matter of the church demanding that people's rights be respected. There is also the question of whether the local Christian community can offer to people a real *experience* of community, a sense that they are respected, that they are loved, that they belong. People in rural areas belong to natural communities so it is easy for them to feel at home. But the masses who are pouring into the cities have no such natural sense of community. Community-building in the urban and suburban situation is a major test for the church. One important way of doing it is to enable people to participate in decision-making. Another is to fight against class distinctions by giving special consideration to those who are poor. In many places the church also has a major role to play at the local level by transcending tribal and racial barriers.

The Challenge of Indigenization and Incarnation

The social and political problems which face the church, although very important, may not be the most basic ones facing the missionary in Africa or Asia. The cultural challenge is at least equally important. That is why I am linking indigenization and "incarnation." Indigenization is the process by which the church becomes truly local. It is usually understood to apply to the replacement of foreign personnel by local people. But this is too limited. One way to widen the concept is to include financial resources. A truly indigenous church should be largely self-supporting. An even more important aspect of indigenization is that the local people should be able to experience the church as truly part of their own history. Christianity must not be seen as merely an imposition from outside, something alien—the white man's religion. Rather the Christian faith has to become "incarnate"; it has to take flesh within the culture of the people. It is true of course that the church challenges aspects of every culture. So there can be no question of the church accepting *all* the values of each new culture it meets. What is needed is a very careful discernment process in which Christians allow the Holy Spirit to teach them which aspects of their culture are to be accepted, which are to be improved, which are to be challenged. There are no ready-made answers to these questions.

It is vitally important that their discernment process take place, and be acted on, in order that all the peoples of the world be given a real opportunity to respond to Christ. Nobody should have to abandon his or her own culture in order to become a Christian. But the "incarnation" of Christian faith in many cultures is also important for another reason; each new embodiment reveals new facets of Christianity. And we will not really know fully what Christ means for the world until his church is "incarnated" in the various cultures of the world. Quite frequently one hears the remark that the safest and best way to ensure that the church take on a truly local character is to wait until local leaders have taken over and then let them decide what elements of the culture can be accepted. But I think this can be used as an easy way for missionaries to avoid facing the tasks that they took on when they set out to bring Christianity to the area. Quite often foreign missionaries are in a better position to judge how inculturation should take place, or at least they ought to be! A missionary is educated to cross the cultural barrier. It is hardly fair to leave the work of "incarnation" to Christians who may have had little experience of other cultures and little opportunity to study church history. The ideal, of course, is a pooling of resources where foreign missionaries and local people all contribute to the discernment process.

I have been extending the meaning of the word "indigenization" to include what I consider the most fundamental aspect of it, namely, the cultural aspect, the "incarnation" of Christian faith in different cultures. But now I want to comment briefly on the more limited meaning of "indigenization," where it refers to the handing over of control to local church leaders. What I find very sad is that the same mistakes can be repeated in diocese after diocese, country after country, continent after continent.

Missionaries (like other human beings!) seem to find it very difficult to learn from the experience of others. There is always the temptation to believe that "our case is different." Perhaps some of the tensions would be lessened by a really good course offered to missionaries on "Stages in the Growth of a Local Church," a course that would be convincing because it would be based on the accumulated experience of hundreds of situations in the present and in the past history of the church.

At this point I am tempted to make one generalization based on my limited experience. I suggest that in general many of the Protestant missionary groups were inclined to indigenize the leadership of the young churches rather too suddenly, while the Catholic church on the other hand has indigenized its leadership rather too slowly. This means that Protestants and Catholics face opposite kinds of problems.

The problems that arise from being too slow in handing over control to local leaders are obvious. Here I merely mention the dangers of paternalism and of frustration. The Catholic church in many missionary areas faces an array of problems in regard to indigenous leadership. The problems do not derive so much from a reluctance to hand over control to local people. The major source of difficulty arises from the limitations of the forms of ministry that are available. I shall return to this point when I consider the challenge of leadership.

Too sudden an indigenization of leadership brings serious problems. These problems faced a number of Protestant churches many years ago. It could easily happen that the same mistakes will now be made in some Catholic mission areas, either because of a shortage of missionaries or because of the unwillingness of some missionaries (for personal or theological reasons) to "stay with" the missionary task they undertook. Where indigenization of leadership takes place too quickly there is one major danger that can give rise to a whole range of practical problems. This is the danger that the new leaders will be unable to distinguish between what is basic in Christianity and the merely accidental trappings of the West.

The Challenge of Dialogue

The third challenge facing the missionary church today is closely related to the challenge of "incarnating" the church in other cultures. It is the challenge of dialogue, taking the word "dialogue" to refer to the specific question of our encounter with groups who differ from us in their religious outlook. I find it helpful to distinguish between dialogue with the world religions, dialogue with traditional religion, dialogue with pentecostalist-prophetic groups, and dialogue with other major Christian churches.

First a brief comment about dialogue with the major world religions. Among the basic issues that arise are two that are particularly urgent today. The first is in what sense can we say that God's word is expressed in the sacred books of the other religions, for instance in the Koran or in the Hindu Scriptures. The second major issue that arises is how are we to understand the uniqueness of Christ. These issues are debated by theologians; but in order that the theological discussions be really significant they need to be underpinned by a dialogue at the grassroots level and by a sympathetic understanding by Christians of the outlook of the people of other religions. It is only when dialogue has taken place at this deep level that there can be an effective entry of the church into the culture of other peoples. The point I am making is that the religion of a people is the deepest and most profound aspect of its culture; so we cannot solve problems of "inculturation" without effective religious dialogue.

There is urgent need for religious dialogue not only with the major world religions like Islam and Hinduism and Buddhism, but also with the traditional religions. But it can be much more difficult to get involved in this kind of dialogue. One reason is that the dialogue must take place to a considerable extent *within* us. This means that we missionaries must really study the religion of the local people. We must be able to sympathize with the kind of questions people are asking. We must not impose our kind of questions on them. For instance, very few people of the traditional religions are asking the question "How many Gods are there?" Rather they are asking practical questions like "Why does this evil occur?" and, "How can I be relieved of this sickness which is oppressing me here and now?" I am afraid that our dialogue with traditional religion has only barely begun. It is very important for us to carry it much further. I would add that the experts in regard to traditional religion are not likely to be scholars reading books but rather people in the field who can really be sensitive to the traditional values of people, to the questions they ask, to the values they have, to their hopes and their fears. It is a matter of great urgency that this kind of dialogue with traditional religion should take place. In fact I believe that it is a precondition for effective "incarnation" of the church. Even where a major world religion has replaced the local traditional religion of an area there still has to be a kind of dialogue with the traditional religion. For the world religions often take over and embody a lot of the traditional religious values of a people.

The third aspect of dialogue that I would like to consider here is dialogue with what I would call the "pentecostalist-prophetic churches." What I have in mind here are the praying and healing churches that have grown up all over Africa and in parts of Asia. They are seldom involved in the ecumenical relationships between the main Christian churches; and some of the more "prophetic" groups have elements that are doubtfully Christian. For these reasons I feel justified in putting them in a separate category. I think there are two reasons for giving them particular attention. First of all, they are often the churches of the poor—of those who have come into the cities and are "on the margins" in many senses. Do we really believe that "salvation comes from the poor"? Secondly, they are interesting and important for us because they can be seen as an amalgam of elements borrowed from different sources. For instance they borrow much of the symbolism of Catholicism—vestments, processions, etc. From the Protestant churches they have taken a great respect for the Bible—sometimes interpreted in a very fundamental way. From the traditional tribal cults they have borrowed or retained certain significant features, e.g., emphasis on being possessed by spirits and emphasis on healing.

Many of these prophetic-pentecostalist churches have sprung up very quickly. So they represent a response to immediate needs of people. By studying how they have responded we can learn a lot about how we ourselves ought to respond. This is not to say that we should make these churches the sole model of what the Catholic church ought to be. In fact frequently they attract only a small proportion of the people. But we have much to learn from them, particularly in the way they can give people a sense of community. We noted earlier (under the heading of the social challenge) how important it is that the people on the margins of the city, and the margins of life, should be given a sense of community.

The final item I wish to refer to under the heading of dialogue is the ecumenical challenge which faces the missionary church. The scandal of disunity and even competition between the churches is so obvious that we tend to get used to it. And that is just the problem. We are no longer overwhelmed with shame that we Western missionaries have exported our divisions and inflicted them on other people. We do not experience the problem with the sense of urgency which it merits. However there are some grounds for hope. As the more evangelical of the Protestant churches have become indigenous in their leadership many of them have abandoned the fanatical anti-Catholicism which characterized their American or European missionaries. On the Catholic side Vatican II has of course given a basis for a far more open approach to the other Christian churches. One notable advance that has resulted is the development of common Christian syllabi for schools, so that Catholic and Protestant pupils can study Christianity together. But at least equally significant is the growing practice of Protestants and Catholics praying together, especially in charismatic prayer meetings. This type of prayer also leads to greater unity between the mainline churches and the pentecostal churches which until recently had little to do with ecumenism.

The Leadership Challenge

I would like now to go on to the fourth major challenge to missionaries today. This is the challenge of leadership. As usually presented the issue is: How do we train leaders? I would like to change it slightly and ask: How does a young church *discover* and train its leaders? Up to the present the missionary churches have had two types of leaders, the catechist type leader and the priest type. The catechist was usually one who had *emerged* already as a leader in the community. But to produce the priests we set up junior and senior seminaries. (Many young churches are now tending to follow this same model in regard to the religious life.) It is a matter of some urgency in most missionary areas to narrow the gap between these two types of leaders—the highly-educated priest trained in Western-style seminaries and living a Western style of life and the almost uneducated catechist who has sprung from the people and lives at their level, but has natural leadership qualities. We need to find new styles of education for the ministry. Think of the ministry of the priest as it is at present as a kind of package; we may have to untie that package to some extent and take some of the activities presently carried out by the priest and allow these to be carried out by lay ministers. This of course has already been done in many areas but we may need to carry it even further. But the main point that I want to make is that we should not approach the question of new ministries independently of the question of education for the ministry, since the two questions are so closely related. I think it is of great importance that those who exercise the priesthood and those who exercise lay ministries (and also people who enter the religious life) should for at least part of their time of training be educated together and learn to work in *teams*.

The Challenge of Building Basic Communities

Very closely related to the question of leadership and teamwork is the fifth challenge for the missionary church today—the challenge posed by the church's recognition of the priority it must give to building basic communities. I need hardly mention that in many missionary areas the church has officially accepted that this must be among its very highest priorities. But it is far easier to set it as a priority than to find ways of doing it in practice. The building of communities is largely a question of animating and evoking involvement of ordinary Christians. Leadership is the crucial factor in building a community; and the leadership that is required is one that involves trusting people and remaining close to them. The leader who wants just to give orders and remain remote or unchallenged will be an obstacle to the building of a community.

The second basic point to be made about community building is that understanding of human development must embrace both the spiritual and the more material aspects. In other words we need an integrated view that includes liberation and development and evangelization; and we have to find a balance between all of these. In some ways it is easier to work out this balance on the ground than it is in the realm of theology. Furthermore it is for the theologians to reflect on what is done in practice rather than to provide a set of instructions coming down from the top. But theology can help to situate the local problems within the wider context of the whole church.

The Challenge to the Missionary: Faith and Trust

Now we come to the last of the six challenges—and this is a different kind of challenge. It is the *personal* challenge that the missionary faces when confronted with the five challenges that I have mentioned already. The five challenges are once again: the social challenge, the challenge of indigenization and incarnation, the challenge of dialogue, the challenge of leadership, and the challenge of building basic communities. These challenges can be experienced by the missionary as a great threat. It is all too easy to become disheartened by the difficulty of doing anything about these enormous problems. So in speaking of the challenge to the missionary I have in mind first of all a challenge of morale and a challenge of faith. Morale and faith are very closely related. In fact I would say that the faith of the missionary is expressed in his or her hope.

The gift of missionary hope is the ability to see the positive aspects of the various challenges that confront us rather than being disheartened by their negative aspects. Hope enables us to see these challenges as areas of growth, areas where we can trust God and trust people. Very basic to missionary spirituality is a readiness to trust the Holy Spirit and to trust the people among whom we work. We do this not by denying the insecurity we feel, but rather by accepting our weakness, accepting our insecurity and in that very helplessness finding our hope. Ultimately, our hope is not built on our own ability, or even on the abilities of the people among whom we work. It is built on God. If we have a great trust in God, a trust in the Spirit to work through others, then we are set free to trust other people without placing too great a weight on them. Our world will not be shattered when others let us down, or even when we ourselves fail, because the foundation of our world is something beyond anything that we find in ourselves or in others. So this personal challenge to the missionary is the challenge of praying for, expecting, and accepting the gift of hope. When it is accepted it finds expression in our *trust* of others.

Trust of people among whom God has called us to live is one of the most fundamental attitudes that must characterize the missionary today. The need for it is well brought out in the following poem written by a bishop from a very poor country. It is addressed to us missionaries and is called "Walk with Us":

Help us to discover our own riches
Don't judge us poor because we lack what you have.

Help us discover our chains
Don't judge us slaves by the type of shackles you wear.

Be patient with us as a people
Don't judge us backward simply because we don't follow your stride.

Be patient with our pace
Don't judge us lazy simply because we can't follow your tempo.

Be patient with our symbols
Don't judge us ignorant because we can't read your signs.

Be patient with us and proclaim the richness of your life
which you share with us.

Be with us and be open to what we can give
Be with us as a companion who walks with us,
Neither behind nor in front
In our search for life and ultimately for God.

Notice especially the request of the poet that we should be *with* his people. This is the final point I would like to stress: what we are challenged to do is to be in *solidarity* with people, above all with people who are poor. We are challenged to be "with" them, to learn from them. We share what we have with them, but dare not presume that we have nothing to receive from them. If I were asked to pick out what I would regard as *the* most fundamental challenge facing missionaries today I would say without any hesitation that it is the challenge to change our attitudes, to break decisively from the Western attitudes of superiority and activism, to learn instead to be in solidarity with the people, to be patient with them and to be prepared to learn from them. Unless we can learn this basic lesson there is no way we can respond effectively to the other challenges—the social challenge, the challenge of indigenization, the challenge of dialogue, the challenge of leadership, and the challenge of building communities. But if we can learn this lesson, respond to this personal challenge of a change of attitude, of a real ongoing conversion, then by the power of God we will be able to answer all the other challenges. We are called to conversion. We must want to be converted; but we must be aware that it comes as a gift from God.

3

THE MESSAGE OF PUEBLA

Marcos McGrath

The Holy Father, speaking to a bishop from Europe about a pastoral assembly he was planning within his diocese, suggested that he carry out the pastoral assembly in the light of Puebla. This is rather startling, but I thing it is an indication of the times that we are living in. Fr. Bühlmann has spoken very eloquently about the Third Church. I think we are beginning to realize the meaning of this Third Church, particularly as it affects us in Latin America—the importance of that large block of Catholics and Christians, the importance of our efforts there to express and live our faith, our gospel, our church, in the midst of the poor and of the poor nations of the world. It is in this sense that I believe Puebla takes on so much significance.

There is so much about Puebla that we could talk about. We could go into the aspects of liberation theology as expressed there and as expressed on our continent: what we mean by evangelizing the poor—the church of the poor being evangelized from the poor—and the whole area of human promotion; the development in our concept of the social teaching of the church, as it is now being called again. There are so many angles, so many points, so many aspects, that we could dwell upon. But what I'd like to do is to present Puebla to you in a fashion that will assist you to read later the document in its English edition and to read it in the context of what is happening in the church and in our peoples of Latin America. Particularly I would like to present this to you from a missionary angle. For that purpose I will begin with some brief remarks about the missionary church. From there I will go on to some remarks concerning the history of the Latin American church, as a missionary church, in order to place us in the context of Puebla.

Theologically and canonically we used to speak of the missionary church in terms of the established church, sending members, personnel, and resources to the church being established in what we generally called "younger areas" and younger churches. The Council has brought us to a deeper concept of the mission of the church and the missionary church. First let us stress that the whole church is missionary—not merely some professionals whom we sup-

Marcos McGrath is the archbishop of Panama City and Vice-President of CELAM.

port and send abroad however effective they may be, but the whole church. The first mission of any local church is its own area and its own people. *Lumen Gentium* points out that the greatest contribution of the local church to the universal church is the vigor of its own inner life. This has brought us in our own times to recognize many areas of missionary action within our local church, and in so doing to discover many aspects of mission action and method which can be applied from the so-called missionary areas to our own countries—what is called reverse mission. In Latin America this concept of missionary church is in a somewhat ambiguous situation. It is at one and the same time an old church going on five centuries of evangelization and also a new church. It is at one and the same time an established church and a missionary church.

The Vatican Council also brings home very strongly to us the fact that the church is not limited to the visible confines of the Roman Catholic communion: it stresses for us that in prayer and action, ecumenism is essential to the efforts of the whole church. Vatican II stresses very much the life of the local church—a concept which has been somewhat lost from view but is coming back with growing strength. Stressing the particularities of the local church brings out more strongly the concept of the whole church—that we are one church throughout the world and that we are responsible for the church throughout the world—not only bishops, but all members of the church. The See of Peter becomes the sign and guarantee of our particularities as local churches as well as our unity as a world communion.

And finally the Vatican Council stresses the concept of the church in the world; this is an essential part of the church's mission at every level—local, national, and international—the promotion of human dignity, the promotion of justice and peace in society, as a reflection of its own inner communion and as a preparation for the world to come. In the light of these conciliar approaches to a deeper concept of missionary church, we look very briefly at the church of Latin America.

The conquest, colonization, and first missionary evangelization of that vast area called Latin America during the sixteenth century were spectacular. It's adventurous reading; it was an adventurous period. It is called by many the heroic age of missionary effort in Latin America—the sixteenth century and the beginning of the seventeenth century. It brought in to being very serious church life. In the early part of the seventeenth century in the then small town of Lima, Peru, there lived five Christians who are now canonized saints of Holy Mother Church. This is remarkable—even more so that one of them was the Archbishop. Nonetheless, during this period there was the unresolved conflict between faith and life, the conflict of the two powers: the power of the sword and commercial enterprise, and the power of the Gospel and the sacrament of the church. And this conflict remained latent as it buried itself within the establishment of the church in Latin America. Between 1650 and 1820 missionary zeal declined; fatigue on the Iberian Peninsula— Spain and Portugal—was felt throughout the colonies of the Americas. But then this declining missionary zeal is also explained by the sense of a church that was already established.

The sense of Christianity has been established in structures: political, ecclesiastical, social, cultural, and religious, which maintain and carry on the forms of Christian life, and can often deceive us as to the real content of that Christian life. The lack of sufficient and genuine kerygma and conversion in the life of a church led to the easy baptism of indigenous populations, and later the populations of the black slaves, without sufficient effort at genuine conversion. Therefore conversions, which involved the whole series of ambiguous positions regarding pagan and superstitious practices, incorporated into or parallel to Christian culture and Christian cult, became projected onto the whole society. It was considered that by simply being born into a Christian society and being baptized, one was necessarily a converted Christian.

In the nineteenth century there was a sharp break with the colonial period, an introduction into a republican period. And because of the divisions within the church and society—particularly within the church, between the higher clergy and the lower clergy, between Spain and the colonies—there was a destructive situation throughout the nineteenth century. This is a period of which very little is said or spoken of or understood by persons viewing Latin America from abroad. But, in a very real sense, many of our problems in Latin America today originated in the nineteenth century. It was during this period that the rather large number of indigenous priests and religious and catechists who existed in our churches was decimated by the closing of the seminaries and the non-functioning of the dioceses and of the convents and of the religious communities, so that by the end of the century we had a very tired church, a very divided church, a very weakened church. It was in 1899 that Pope Leo XIII convoked that first and only synod of all the Latin American bishops. And it is from this date that we can really talk of the second foundation of the church in Latin America. From a missionary point of view this is extremely important if one wants to understand the background of the people about whom one is speaking and with whom one is working.

Church history can be viewed very effectively and very fruitfully within the context of the great councils in church history. And certainly one of these great councils was the Second Vatican Council. I think that council had its preparatory time roughly beginning with the advent of Pope Leo XIII to the throne of Peter. We can talk therefore about the modern history of the church of Latin America with the preparation of the Second Vatican Council. Latin America was brought into the full flow of this preparation by the synod in 1899 and we find ourselves—the church of Latin America—being given constant impulses forward by the Holy Father in Rome during the early part and the middle part of this century. And so under Pope Pius X and successive popes we have the beginnings and the stirrings in Latin America of some sense of lay participation leading later into Catholic action; some sense of sacramental, liturgical life leading to the full-blown liturgical movement; the beginnings of a return to Scripture leading to the biblical movement; some theological reflection leading eventually into our present theological contributions; and the beginnings of a social movement in our church and even some appearance of ecumenism.

In the 1930s we find very active movements in our churches in many parts of Latin America. It is the revived church coming out of the structures, coming into the new world, that begins to make itself present in the changing society of Latin America. In the 1940s, after the Second World War, Latin America experienced a strong economic recession: great poverty, flight from the land to the cities, the beginning of those belts of poverty, those slums around our cities which are the life of modern poverty—a new kind of poverty affecting our people. In this situation Christians began to feel more deeply the need for Gospel and a Christian life that speaks to the poor and speaks to the injustices and the miseries of our people. It was then that we had the multiplication of social action groups, based upon the Gospel and Christian living, and the beginning of many labor unions and political parties that were Christian and Gospel-inspired. All of this led to a new kind of church in Latin America; from the missionary point of view, it is extremely interesting. It is a church which is questioning itself, asking itself whether or not the established Christianity is really what it seems to be. And this was truly a preparation for the Council: our sharing in the preparation for the Council which caused us to question ourselves and question the whole universal church as to whether or not we were really present in, and serving, the modern world with the Gospel and the sacrament of the Lord.

It is interesting that in this period of the forties, the fifties, the sixties and thereafter, we began to receive from many parts of the world, particularly Western Europe and North America, new missionary systems. The attention of the Western church became focused on Latin America, and thousands upon thousands of missionaries came to our assistance and millions and millions of dollars were poured into the church of Latin America. This is a sign of mission awareness in the universal church focused upon our area of the world and at the same time it is a sign in our area of our need. It came at such a propitious moment that it gave the church of Latin America, and continues to give us, an ability to respond to our problems that certainly we would not have had without all this assistance. But this great input from abroad has forced us also to ask ourselves what we are. Faced with so many different pastoral approaches coming from so many different areas, the church of Latin America looks for its self-identification. And it wants to know itself more and more and be able to respond, apostolically and even economically, to absorb aid from abroad and make it its own life. Rome assists in this process and Rome encourages the bishops of Latin America, so that when the Eurcharistic Congress was held in Rio in 1955 the bishops afterwards held a first General Council of Latin American Bishops which created CELAM. At the beginning CELAM was made up of one delegate from each Latin American country or episcopal conference. With a general secretary and assistant in Bogotá, and a president elected from its members, it rather timidly sought its way at the start—from 1955 until the beginning of the Council. But in the Council it found itself, because there at the Council we ourselves from Latin America (I had been consecrated a bishop the year before the Council) were surprised at our input into the Council as were most of the others there present. And also in the setting of the Council, of the world problems of the church, we became more aware of ourselves as Latin American. CELAM was the natural instrument for the co-ordination of many, many meetings of bishops from Latin America who prepared the themes of the Council. At the same time CELAM became the inspiration for the continuation of these meetings in our own environment after the Council.

So it was from 1964 on that CELAM began to promote specialized meetings on the application of the Council, but at a Latin American level. This was very significant. For the first time we were bringing together our best theologians, our best pastoral leaders, our best liturgists, with bishops, lay persons, and religious, to consider on a Latin American level the problems of our church. This was inspiring, most invigorating, and began to give some pastoral lines which were helpful to us all. Pope Paul VI followed us closely and three weeks before the Council ended, he gave a talk to all the bishops of Latin America assembled in the Vatican and spoke to us of CELAM as a providential instrument given to us by the Lord which we should utilize to obtain a pastoral plan for the whole of Latin America. This was tremendous —a pastoral plan for the whole of Latin America. Who speaks of a pastoral plan for the whole of Europe or a pastoral plan for the whole of Africa or the whole of Asia or even the whole of North America? This could only be made possible by the certain common bonds which hold us together, as a people of Latin American—the large nation of Latin America. It could only be made possible by the encouragement of the Holy Father of the universal church and it has become more and more a reality.

On the continent which needs so much to be integrated, which is so divided by political and economic factors, the most uniting and integrating force is certainly the church. After the Council these specialized meetings continued, sponsored by the new departments set up by CELAM in these various areas of liturgy, social action, catechesis, and so forth. And as they began to produce more and more guidelines, suddenly the thought appeared, well why not have a general meeting about the application of the Council to Latin America? And thus the second General Conference of Latin American Bishops in Medellín took shape. It was approved by the Holy Father and rather quickly prepared in January 1968. The presidents of CELAM with a few other members put together a first document and sent it to all the episcopal conferences who in turn sent back their brief responses. In May of that year a work-document was put together and sent back to them, and this was the beginning of the basic text which we brought to our meeting in August when the Holy Father Paul VI inaugurated Medellín in Bogotá. We then transferred ourselves to the city of Medellín, met for two weeks, and put out sixteen documents that are now known as the documents of Medellín.

Medellín did not attract very much attention in itself—it was simply a meeting of bishops of Latin America to apply the Council. It didn't have much press attention—there were about eighty or ninety press people, which at the time seemed a great number—but Medellín was called in football terms a "sleeper." It began to attract attention as these documents spread about and as they were read and it became obvious that this had become a very prophetic moment for the church in Latin America—the first time on any continent that the bishops had come together to speak so emphatically about innovation and change in the three areas touched upon: human promotion, development in the faith, and church structures. It emphatically denounced defects in all of these areas, and strongly called for reform, for change, for justice, for better church effort in so many areas. It is important to note this because it was the success of Medellín—the prophetic success of Medellín—which is taken into consideration by so many in judging Puebla. After eight years of living Medellín, which in itself was the application of the Council to Latin America, the thought began to occur among the bishops of Latin America that it would be well after ten years to have a Third General Conference of Latin American Bishops to ask ourselves where we are, where we are going, how are the Council and Medellín being applied in our continent?

As soon as this was mentioned, sectors of the press, sectors of the European, African, North American, and Asian churches, and of course sectors of the Latin American church, began to ask: Is this going to be a prolongation, a continuation, a deepening of Medellín, or is this going to be an empty Medellín to turn the clock back? Are the conservatives going to try to stop what is happening in the church in Latin America? The answer to these questions became quite obvious after a year of preparation for Puebla. Puebla was approved by the Holy Father as a Third General Conference on the theme of "evangelization in Latin American in the present and in the future" in January of 1977. And immediately preparation began. It was a broader preparation than had been the case with Medellín. This was because we had learned more about consultation and participation in the church. That was what we had been learning—Medellín was still learning years after the Council.

The post Vatican II synods have taught us more about consultation, as have parish, diocesan, national, and pastoral councils. So in approaching Puebla it was impossible not to have a vast consultation and it was a help. During 1977 there were meetings of bishops from all over the continent, as well as meetings of priests, of religious, of lay persons. We had a round of regional meetings of bishops' delegates from each of the countries. The lay movements met, the religious conferences met, and all this was fed into CE-LAM, which had the statutory task of preparing Puebla. From this came a first consultative document which was sent to the bishops at the end of 1977, and put into consultation from January 1978 on. In some areas it was torn to ribbons, it was criticized, it was taken apart, and barely put back together again. And this was the finest thing that could have happened because it was the first project, a first draft of what could be a working document.

Between January and June of 1978, the consultation went much more deeply into the basic Christian communities, the parishes, the dioceses, the movements. Through the whole month of July 1978 a team of bishops with Cardinal Lorsheider, the president of CELAM, and a small group of secretaries and technicians put together a working document which really became a collection of the voluminous and rich contributions especially of the episcopal conferences but also of the whole life of the church in Latin America. This working document was sent out to all the bishops in time for the conference which was to have taken place in October 1978 but was postponed until the end of January because of the deaths of the two Holy Fathers.

The important thing about the preparation was that this consultation brought out the riches of church life in Latin America. And it is this life, the ongoing process of application of council renewal, that made it impossible to move back from Medellín. What had been started in Medellín so prophetically had been repeated thousands and thousands of times in Latin America and could not be undone. And many of the recommendations of Medellín had become realities in our lives. We were no longer talking about founding basic Christian communities—they existed all round us, they exist all around us. Now we were talking about greater participation of the laity in the ministerial life of the church and we had hundreds of thousands of delegates of the Word, straining towards a greater participation in the evangelizing mission of the church. We were no longer talking about the great incorporation of religious into the life of the local church. In my own archdiocese of Panama, where before we had no religious sisters working in basic communities, we now have twenty-seven groups working in the poorest areas, on the land, in the city, in the slum areas. These are now realities.

We are no longer talking about a church which tries to identify itself more with the poor. The church in Latin America has become more and more of the poor, and with the poor, not universally, not uniformly in all areas, but more and more so. And this has been manifested in many parts of Latin America.

The celebration of Puebla took place with the spectacular arrival of Pope John Paul II to Mexico. His coming was of great importance—his presence, his personality, and his message. His presence demonstrated the importance of the church of Latin America and of this conference for the church of Latin America. He transferred the See of Rome to Mexico for one week and he gave so many talks that he really constructed a magisterium around this event of Puebla. In his personality there was combined a strong sense of his role as Holy Father with a simplification of protocol and a very immediate communicative contact with the people. At the end of the week the president of Mexico said, "I must tell you legislators that I am the president of a secular state but I am also the president of a believing people"—an extraordinary statement in the Mexican context.

But his message was also very telling. He brought to us immediately a strong Marian piety, a strong accenting of popular religious values in our people, combined with a strong insistence on conciliar renewal. The old and the new—the old renewed, the old brought to new life. He stressed a great deal the original message of the Gospel: that neither Christ nor the church is to be reduced to a solely economic system or political message or party. At the same time this Gospel message, in all of its import and application, must constantly be brought to bear upon human dignity on every level. Never has a pope spoken to us as strongly as he spoke to us in Mexico, addressing himself to the bishops and then to the people of Mexico, regarding the necessity of Christian action for social justice.

That some newspaper reports took his talk to us as a rejection of social action on the part of the church, or as a condemnation of liberation theology, was a great falsification. They simply took a few of his statements from the first part of his talk entirely out of context. If one reads the entire speech (his speech is printed sometimes with parts left out), and if one not only reads that speech but the rest of his speeches in Mexico, one will see that John Paul II gave tremendous impulse to the presence of the church in the defense of human dignity in all areas. He stressed and spelled out for us the violations of human dignity taking place in Latin America in such a way that we cannot remain silent in the face of these violations of human rights.

You will find in the first part of the document of Puebla what is called the pastoral description of the reality of Latin America. It is just not any kind of description—it is a pastoral description. Now this is a very fine and delicate distinction but a very important and a very real distinction. We spent two years, beside all the previous investigation and study, receiving reports and going over reports about the economic, the social, the political, and cultural situation of our countries and of our continent. But we were not called upon to speak as economists, or as politicians, or as any kind of social scientists: we were speaking as pastors. This I think is a good pattern for us. We should know the economic problems we are going to talk about, but in order to talk about them as pastors. The description of the reality of Latin America brings out, first of all, the historical period to which I made reference. Secondly, it brings out the social, cultural, and political realities, stressing the fact that although Latin America has increased its economic welfare in an overall sense, it has not known how to distribute this increased wealth to its population. So we have a greater separation between rich and poor than we had on our continent ten years ago, and more misery and injustice.

There is the political possibility of overcoming these situations in Latin America, because wealth is there, but there is the lack of a political will—and a lack of a moral will—and it is the role of the church to encourage this will by becoming the voice of the voiceless—those who cannot protest the injustice to which they are subjected. This does not place the whole blame upon international structures. Much of the blame is within our own national structures and basically in our own hearts. But it certainly does connect the international to the national structures that maintain these mechanisms of oppression, as Pope John Paul II called them.

The description of the religious reality takes into view the growth, the life of the church in Latin America since the Council. The reality of this development along the lines of a renewed church is what gives hope to the church of Latin America and what reaffirms the basic lines of the Council and Medellín and projects towards the future.

It is against this background in the first part of the document that in the second part we go on to the message itself: the design of the Father for Latin America; the Gospel, but the Gospel message preached not in a void but preached to our people today in Latin America; the return to the sources, but the taking of these sources to our people in their situation. In this second part there is, first of all, the content of the message, and then there is the communication of the message. In the content there is stress upon the truth about Christ, the truth about the church, and the truth about humankind—the tripod as we came to call it—which Pope John Paul II stressed in his opening address. In the first two chapters, on truth about Christ and the church, one would expect to find a rather developed presentation of Latin American theology, christology, and ecclesiology. The basic gains in this theology are presented there, particularly the emphasis upon the historical Christ, upon the historical following of Christ, upon the church following in the way of Christ, in its suffering and in its taking upon itself the plight of the poor and making that plight its own, through the cross to redemption. Nonetheless there are many aspects of liberation which are not explicitly contained in these chapters for the very obvious reason that this is a new development in theology in Latin America, and has to mature. The Holy Father himself indicated a few corrective lines of thought without condemning, and Puebla follows in the same direction.

It has been said, I think with justice and reason, that the christology and ecclesiology in the pastoral sections of this document of Puebla are much richer than the christology and ecclesiology in the two chapters explicitly dedicated to this purpose. For we are living these realities; we have not yet been able to think them out, to spell them out, clearly incorporating the reservations and corrections which are necessary for precise statements of Catholic truth in our present circumstance.

The third chapter—the emphasis upon truth about man—is extremely important. The Holy Father has given great weight to it in all of his statements and it is one of the singular contributions of Puebla to the advancement of Christian social teaching. The Christian doctrine about humanity as a foundation of our Christian social teaching (the Holy Father stressed this) is brought in very well in this document and into the part in reference to evangelization, human promotion, and the development of a dynamic social teaching for our times.

The second section of this—the second part of the message—the design of God for his people in Latin America, is a treatise in five parts on evangelization developed in a fashion which is extremely helpful for us because it takes *Evangelii Nuntiandi* and many of the church documents that are so rich and it puts them in the context of our church in Latin America.

The third part of the document is concerned about evangelizing the church itself. This has been stressed in *Evangelii Nuntiandi,* and it is perhaps the most important aspect of our church today—the evangelizing, the conversion of the church itself. Without this conversion we continue the myth that we are already an established church and that all we have to do is to continue to sacramentalize ourselves and to present ourselves to the world.

Then we come to the fourth part, which is also the area of pastoral directives, namely, the missionary church of Latin America—and it is very interesting that the term "missionary" is used in that title. The church addressing itself to the world does so as a missionary church and at the same time recognizes that the world is a pluralistic society. The first chapter in this part speaks of action for the poor—the preferential action of the Latin American church for the poor—and I say the Latin American church because these are our poor, and this is our situation. This formula cannot easily be applied to other parts of the world because there are different priorities, but certainly in Latin America the poor are our priority. And then there is the action for the young in a continent of young people.

Next there is a singularly new approach: the evangelization of the constructors of the pluralist society. We have come to realize that evangelization cannot be generic, cannot be simply preaching the Gospel in dioceses and parishes and in basic communities on a geographical basis. We must bring the Gospel into dialogue with the constructors of a modern pluralistic society, which is to say, our student leaders, our politicians, our labor leaders, our farm leaders. The Gospel must be dialogued with persons in all of these areas if it is to be incorporated into them, so that we can bring Christian principles and values into these structures of a pluralistic society.

Finally, the last chapter concerns itself with the defense of human dignity on a national and on an international plane, though much of what the church has been doing in the last fifteen years has been taken up and projected forward, and particularly given an international value and world scope that it did not previously have.

The theme of Puebla is expressed in these terms: evangelization towards communion and participation—but an evangelization which is a liberating evangelization. Liberation is first of all for each person from the weight of sin; evangelization means necessarily personal conversion or it has not had any effect, and this is the first liberation which then takes us into the liberation of humankind from all of these things which weigh upon us. In the pluralistic society which characterizes the world today, Christians are to be a leaven toward communion and participation of all in a more equal and just society.

I think Puebla, having brought upon itself the attention of the universal church, has made us more aware and conscious of the fact that we as a church in Latin America are appearing on the world scene, perhaps for the first time, with new responsibilities. But we are very conscious, as all of this process of Medellín and Puebla and before and after are pointing out, of our many, many failings. Above all I think we are arriving at the ability to examine those failings and to realize that we are far from being the established church that we thought we were; that we must be converted; that we are a missionary church; but at the same time that all of us in many ways are missionary churches and that the relationship of our churches in the world today is a mutual missionary relationship. The whole church is a mission in which we share together and in which we are responsible one for another.

4

THE CHURCH IN LATIN AMERICA

José Comblin

We are the collaborators of the Latin American church, but in spite of that condition the Latin American bishops claimed in Puebla that they need and that their church needs a new evangelization, a re-evangelization. Why and in what sense a "new evangelization"? It is because of the specific condition of the Christian faith in Latin America: the existence of a deep and structural contradiction between religion and action, between faith and practice, and such a contradiction had its origins in the beginnings of evangelization. From the beginning, evangelization was a contradiction in Latin America, because evangelization followed the conquest, and the church was divided between one part which was the church of the "conquistadores," and another part which accepted responsibility for defending the human and social rights of the indigenous people. One part of the church was for the indigenous people—the Indians—and the other part represented the oppressors or conquerors. And such a division between two parts of the Catholic church has been the deep and structural contradiction within the Latin American church since the sixteenth century.

There was a permanent debate in the sixteenth and seventeenth centuries between two categories of missionaries on this question of human rights, and such a debate continued until the suppression of the Society of Jesus. The Jesuits were expelled from Latin America: from Brazil in 1859 and from Spanish America between 1863 and 1867. The Jesuits were the traditional defenders of the rights of the Indians and with them were members of other congregations, but the struggle between diocesan priests and the Jesuits worsened the deep contradiction within the Catholic church. And since the eighteenth century the Latin American church remained silent. That was in another sense the church of silence, the silent church, which could not accept the original contradiction and so remained silent about the social problems, about the social application, the social action, the human reality of the Christian faith. Some of the missionaries were also defenders of the slaves, but there was really no possibility of creating a permanent church for defending

Fr. José Comblin is a priest of the diocese of Malines, Belgium, and professor of pastoral theology at the Universities of Talca, Chile, and Louvain, Belgium.

the rights of the slaves. All the missionaries who defended such rights were immediately expelled. Any kind of defense of the slaves was impossible. A kind of defense of the Indians was possible until the eighteenth century so that the first challenge of evangelization was, for the prophetical part of the church, the question of human rights. To a degree the modern problem of human rights was born in America, and articulated in the faculties of theology in Spain just around such debates. Can we, may we, oppress the Indians? Have the American Indians human rights?—that is the real historical origin of the modern Western problem of human rights and the liberal revolutions, and the liberal ideology. So that in Latin America it has been not only a theoretical problem; it has been the deep reality of the church from the beginning. Now this problem was silent and remained silent until this century. In this century there is a new prophetical spirit due partly to the memory of the Second World War and of course stimulated by Vatican Council II. We are now in a renewal of the primitive contradiction of the first kind and it is significant that the Episcopal Conference in Puebla begins recording, remembering, the origins of such contradiction. "We want to repeat, to accept the challenge of the Latin American church in the sixteenth century and we want to repeat their response."

The problem in Latin America is that the oppressors and the oppressed are Christian. The persons who apply torture and the tortured persons are Christian; they are members of the church and that is simply a contradiction. How is it possible for a system of oppression to exist in order to defend the Christian church and the Christian faith? Torture in itself is a part of the human condition; the problem is torture in the name of God, in the name of the church, in the name of Christian civilization. That is the problem of Latin America and therefore the problem is not just to say "there are poor." Of course, there are poor people all over the world, in all countries, but in Latin America the oppressors of the poor are Christians. For two centuries they could rely on the official legitimization of the church, the bishops, and the whole Catholic system—from the eighteenth century up to now. The problem of the new evangelization of Latin America is the problem of action, Christian action, of continuity between faith and action and a real transformation of society in a Christian sense according to the requirements of Christian faith.

The Latin American church has defined itself now clearly in two episcopal conferences, in Medellín in 1968 and in Puebla, in February of 1979, and there is a clear and evident continuity between the documents of both. There is one line, one official line in the Latin American church, and that line is a prophetical line—clearly defined. Of course, in practice this does not say that the whole Latin American church is working in the same direction, but officially it has adopted the line of the prophetical missionaries, invoked by Pope John Paul II in his first speech after landing in Santo Domingo. He cited the famous missionaries of the sixteenth century, the defenders of the Indians, Bartolomé de las Casas and others, so that the official line of the Latin

American bishops is the line of the missionaries in the sixteenth century—the defenders of the human rights of the Indians. This involves several aspects. In the first place, priority for the poor. Who are the poor in Latin America? Poverty is not only a material condition, it is a condition of marginalization. That is to say, in Latin America, development is based on 20 percent of the population—the others do not exist. They are the poor, the non-existing persons, the never-considered persons. They are considered in international meetings but in their countries they do not exist. They exist just as a danger, they exist for the police, the armed forces, but for the progress of the nation they do not exist. That is just the reason for such a commitment of the church, that is, to be the voice of the voiceless, the famous formula of Helder Camara adopted by Pope John Paul II in his speeches in Mexico. The voiceless are 80 percent of the population of Latin America.

Secondly, the commitment to the poor is not passive; it is a requirement for action, real action. The church has no power, no strength, no economic possibility, but it has the possibility of speaking and creating a new consciousness, a new awareness so that the masses, the poor people, become conscious and able to act and become active members of the community. Such inner transformation of the masses from passive subjects to active contributors, active members, sharing a real participation in society is the second commitment of the Latin American church. Such a line was totally confirmed in Puebla with the same words, the same themes, the same specific definition, the same language as that of Medellín. And despite many campaigns, national and international, against the church and against such a commitment of the church to the poor, there is nevertheless an evident and clear continuity between the conference of Puebla and the conference of Medellín.

The poor until twenty years ago were far from the priest; there was never a parish for the poor people, never a religious house or convent for them, and twenty years ago in the countryside, and in the poorer parts of the cities, there were no priests or religious for the poor—they did not exist for the church. They did not exist for society, but now they exist. More and more there are religious communities, communities of priests, and lay people in the midst of the poor. That is the transformation of recent years that received a clear confirmation from the bishops in Medellín and Puebla. Such movement is also a geographical movement from the rich sectors of society to the poor sectors of society, and this movement is one of the most important characteristics of the Latin American church. A real conversion of religious congregations, dioceses, and parishes after an inner struggle provoked this movement from the rich sectors to the poor sectors of the population.

The creation of a new kind of Christian community where the poor people became subjects of their history—that is the meaning of basic Christian community. The best communities are simply communities of poor, based on that commitment. The poor become the active members. For them there is a new reality. Their Christianity was passive in many things; it remained in the family and there was never participation in public life. Now through the basic communities they are active members of the Christian church and they are learning how to become active members of society. That is only a first step, but the challenge is now the complete passivity of the Christian masses, who accept their condition, because the worst condition of slaves is to accept their slavery. That is the first problem, and of course the church cannot give them freedom, political liberation. But the church can give them a consciousness: that they must not accept such a condition; that they may struggle and ask for liberation; that there is no contradiction between God and freedom; that the real God of the Bible is not the God of slaves; that God is not the God who wants their bondage as slaves in Egypt. Rather, the message of God is a message of freedom, of liberty. This is a new message because since the eighteenth century the poor never heard of such a message. The message of the preachers was always patience, resignation, the will of God.

The church has officially now accepted the condition of being the voice of the voiceless, defender of human rights. There is a long struggle ahead: Latin America is now entering the third colonial domination. After the Spanish-Portuguese conquest Latin Americans became in the last century members of the British economic empire. And in this century they are secondary members of the American empire, so that they have very little possibility of an independent economic system. The economy in Latin America is totally dependent on the American system. Culture is totally dependent also; there is no political independence of course; and the dependence is increasing more and more. The present evolution is toward more domination from the Western economy and political system. There is no hope for an immediate liberation; liberation is for the twenty-second century. But the message of the church is to be with the poor at such a time—in their condition of dependence, slavery, oppression—and not to be with the rich, with the oppressors; not to be sharing the feasts of the rich, but the struggles and the sufferings of the poor, those sufferings and those struggles which have gone on for generations. The problem is patience, but active patience, not passive patience. Active with the hope of a possible liberation and in protest, a permanent protest against such a condition, just because such a condition is imposed in the name of God.

The problem in Latin America is one of two Gods or two images of God. There is no atheism but there are two kinds of religions: the God of the Bible, and the God of power and domination. The church is officially defined as a church of the poor but with the temptation of being manipulated by the rich. This temptation is ever-present. Far from Latin America it is easy to resist, but inside, within Latin American society, it is very difficult to defend oneself against the temptation of being seduced by the established system and society and to remain permanently with the poor suffering people who have so little hope of immediate liberation yet have the permanent hope of the Jewish people who waited forty years in the desert. In Latin America we have waited for more than forty years, but now we are waiting with an active patience and active commitment in spite of such domination.

We want to be with the poor people, the slaves, the 50 percent of the Latin

American population who have no prospects of a permanent job. Eighty percent of the population are now living in oppressive conditions. The worst of all is that their dominators are Christian people, Christian people educated in Christian colleges, in Christian universities by Christian priests in Christian parishes and so on. That is the challenge of the Latin American church.

5

THE FUTURE OF MISSION IN ASIA

Parmananda Divarkar

If it is always hazardous to play the prophet, the risk increases enormously when one attempts to forecast what the future has in store for the largest and most diversified continent on the globe, whose missionary history is as old as the church itself. Indeed the church was born and received its mission from the Lord in Asia, in Palestine.

Even if you think only of the East—as is often done when Asia is mentioned, and as we shall generally do in this paper—even thinking only of the East, we have to remember that there is a well established tradition according to which at least one and perhaps two of the apostles who first received the mission from Christ penetrated as far as India. St. Thomas reached the south of the peninsula coming by sea and St. Bartholomew travelled by land and arrived in the north. In spite of this long and glorious history the Christian mission in Asia has made remarkably little headway. As you are aware the only nation that is notably Christian in Asia is the Philippines, and the Philippines resembles more Latin America than the rest of Asia, at least in this respect. If figures are any indication (and they cannot altogether be ignored), Asia is the continent where Christians are proportionately least in the total population. As far as Catholics are concerned, according to a rough calculation, they are 2.5 percent of the total population in Asia, as compared with 13 percent in Africa, 25 percent in Oceania, 40 percent in Europe and 62 percent in the Americas.

Moreover, in not a few Asian countries where the church is fairly well established, the Christian community is not fully integrated into the life of the nation. Many studies have been made of the seemingly poor success of the mission in Asia, and there is much earnest effort being made to determine how one can and should go about the task in the years to come.

We shall attempt here to review some aspects of past history and of the actual situation that may enable a discerning audience to form an idea of what the future will or at least could be.

The missionary effort that has significantly affected the present state and

Fr. Parmananda Divarkar is a Jesuit priest from India and a member of the General Superiors Council in Rome.

future prospects of the church in Asia is the one that goes no farther back than the sixteenth century and was spearheaded by St. Francis Xavier. It expanded in the course of some two hundred years, keeping pace with the extension of Western supremacy in the East. After Europe had been through the crisis of several revolutions, it experienced a great revival with the rise of many new missionary institutes in the nineteenth century. At this time there was also an upsurge of missionary zeal in the churches of the Reformation. Today as we look back at this long period of striving to spread the faith in Asia we can distinguish a difference of approach, or at least a shift in accent between the earlier and the later stages, say, between the sixteenth and seventeenth centuries and the nineteenth and twentieth centuries. Speaking very much in general, it could be said that in the beginning the effort was directed to saving souls by bringing people, whether individuals or groups, into the church as it already existed in the West—with its language, liturgy, laws and devotional practices. It was in this church alone with its rigid structures adopted after the Council of Trent that one could find salvation. It is true that as early as 1659 the newly established Congregation for the Propagation of the Faith issued instructions to the Vicars Apostolic of China giving clear directives for missionaries with regard to the people they were evangelizing. I quote just a brief passage which is rather well known, but I think bears repetition. This is what the congregation said in 1659.

> Do not waste your zeal or your powers of persuasion in getting these people to change their rites, customs or ways of life, unless these be very obviously opposed to faith or morals, for what could be more ridiculous than to import France, Spain, Italy, or any other part of Europe into China? What you carry with you is not a national culture but a message which does not reject, or offend, the sound traditions of any country, but rather wants to safeguard and foster them.

This sounds as enlightened as could be, but in fact at about the same time the brave attempt of Matthew Ricci to build up a truly Chinese Christian way of life was misunderstood and condemned in Rome. The experiment of Robert de Nobili in India along similar lines met the same fate.

Perhaps it could not be otherwise, given the very limited knowledge and comprehension in those days of diversity of cultures. In the early part of the present century with better means of communication and the development of the social sciences both knowledge and understanding had greatly progressed, and many efforts were made to adhere to the principles enunciated by the Congregation of Propaganda.

It was then said that missionary effort was not directed to bringing people into an already established and largely foreign church, but rather to bringing the church to the people and establishing it in their midst, making the necessary adjustments in externals so that it was at home in its surroundings and the people themselves felt at home in it. In our seminary days, we were told that the missionary should not think so much of making converts as of planting the church.

Adaptation, as this concept of evangelization was often called, was a great step forward, but the actual progress was minimal, and this for many reasons. As a matter of fact the changes that were made were very limited in scope and touched only the marginal aspects of Christian life.

The ultimate point of reference in introducing any new feature was neither the Christian faith as such, nor the local culture, but the tradition and practice of the Western church. This was regarded as the model to be adhered to as closely as possible, and was also the standard for judging what was or was not essential to the Christian life, and what was or was not acceptable in the culture of the people. Moreover, a maximum of uniformity was still regarded as an ideal.

It might almost be said that instead of an intimate and fruitful dialogue between faith and culture such as is envisaged by Pope Paul VI in his apostolic exhortation *Evangelii Nuntiandi* there was a monologue by the interpreter. The fact that evangelization was mostly carried on under the protection of the colonial powers almost inevitably fostered a sense of superiority in missionaries, with regard not so much to their personal worth as to the ideas and ways in which they had been brought up. It is easy for us now to find fault with such a mentality, but the attitude is understandable in the ecclesiastical climate that prevailed until the middle of the present century. It seems incredible that as late as 1890 the Congregation of Propaganda gave an answer to a bishop in China that was directly opposed to its own enlightened statement of policy that we quoted earlier. This bishop presented the following problem:

It is repugnant to Chinese culture to manifest affection in public. Hence in the celebration of marriage it is embarrassing for the couple to join hands; since this does not in any way belong to the essence of the sacrament, could it be omitted?

It is bad enough that the question had to be asked at all but the answer was far worse though it was regarded at the time as very gracious. This was the answer that the poor bishop got. He was told that he might for the present tolerate not joining hands but with the understanding that gradually the people must be encouraged to accept the prescriptions of the Roman ritual.

Now comes my second point: some reflections on the situation. Today, reflecting on the policies of the past and their results in the present, it seems inadequate to conceive of the object of mission as planting the church. For in practice, that means rather transplanting it from one place to another, with hardly more than the minimal adjustments required to enable it to survive in its new environment. In fact it has been said that the missionary effort in Asia has produced Christian communities that are like isolated potted plants that may serve a decorative purpose and perhaps embellish the statistical tables of foreign missionary societies, but have not the vitality to make an impact on their own immediate surroundings. This is a harsh and much too sweeping statement, but it does point to a sad truth and to a serious problem. In any case the concern should not be the passing of judgment on the past, but planning hopefully for the future.

In this spirit and keeping to the analogy of the tree as the Gospel itself suggests it, we would say that in order to be healthy and fruitful, the church must submit to the laws of life and grow gradually from a seed. The task of the missionary is to sow the good seed of the word of God. Falling on good soil, this seed will sprout and grow into a tree which will be the local church; that is, it will be a community of believers sharing the same divine life as other similar communities, since it comes from the same Godly seed, but having an appearance all its own, and markedly different from that of others, according to the particular circumstances of its birth and development. Casting its roots deep into the ground, such a tree can spread its branches wide and harbor a great variety of birds—even some strange specimens perhaps! The first plenary assembly of the Federation of Asian Bishops' Conferences meeting in Taipei in April 1974 obviously had such a church in mind when it stated:

> The local church is a church incarnate in a people: a church in continuous, humble and living dialogue with the living traditions, the culture, the religions, in brief with all the life-realities of the people in whose midst it has sunk its roots deeply. It seeks to share in whatever truly belongs to that people: its meaning and its values; its aspirations; its thoughts and its languages.

In saying this the Asian bishops were anticipating by more than a year what Pope Paul said when in *Evangelii Nuntiandi* he formulated the theological position of the church since the Second Vatican Council. These are Pope Paul's words:

> This universal church is in practice incarnated in the individual churches made up of such and such an actual part of mankind, speaking such and such a language, heirs to a cultural patrimony, to a vision of the world, to a historical past, to a particular human substratum. Receptivity to the wealth of the individual church corresponds to a special sensitivity of modern man.

Moreover the pope points out that:

> The local church has the task of proclaiming the good news to the people among whom it is established. It may need help from outside in order to carry out its mission but the responsibility for effective evangelization rests with the local church.

Again Pope Paul:

> The individual churches, intimately built up, not only of people but of aspirations, of riches and limitations, of ways of praying, of loving, of looking at life and the world, which distinguishes this or that human gathering, have the task of assimilating the essence of the Gospel message, and of transposing it without the slightest betrayal of its essential truth into the language that these particular people understand, then of proclaiming it in this language.

The pope goes on in *Evangelii Nuntiandi* to draw attention to the many hazards and very delicate nature of this task—of transposing what he calls the essential truth of the Gospels into a local cultural context.

The difficulty that the pope points out is aggravated in Asia by the fact that there is not just one local situation to be considered; by this I do not mean that in different parts of Asia there are different cultural situations—that is obvious—what I mean is that in the same place one finds co-existing several cultures. For instance in my own India the overwhelmingly prevalent culture is Hindu and this embraces two large ethnic and linguistic groups, the Travanian and the Aryan. But earlier than either of these and still very prominent are the Aboriginals or tribals with their own cultural tradition; later than all these came Moslem culture. The Aboriginals and Moslems each claims more than a tenth of the population and together they make up one-fourth.

And now I come to the third part: What conclusion could be drawn from this situation, and these problems? Prescinding from the more practical problems such as I have just mentioned is of course a basic difficulty in this transposition of the faith in cultural terms. And it is that the essence of our faith is not some abstract formula but the concrete historical reality of Jesus of Nazareth. Can we ignore the Jewishness of Jesus and of the Gospel in our efforts to incarnate the faith in a culture that is so very different from the one of Palestine two thousand years ago? Obviously we cannot do that, yet we must remember that Jesus of Nazareth did himself transcend his historical particularity by dying and rising again to a new kind of life, to be Christ the Lord, the savior of the world.

Now the question I ask is this: If the word of God made flesh died and rose to a new life to save humankind, is it too rash to propose that the word of God, which is the message of salvation, must in some sense die in order to produce a community of those that are saved? It does indeed sound shocking to say that the Gospel, the Good News, must die. But after all it is Our Lord himself who has said that the grain must die in order to bear fruit. In dying the seed does not lose its life but brings it to fullness by communicating it to the tree. It is very well for me to speak like this, but whatever may be the value of this argument, it is certainly not clear what is the practical conclusion to be drawn—what is the application of this argument to the concrete situation.

What I would like to do is to pursue this line a little further, and to suggest that it leads to an understanding of evangelization as dialogue.

This understanding of evangelization as dialogue is, as I hope to show, of particular importance and relevance to Asia.

In any true dialogue as in true love, there is a dying to self until one finds oneself more fully in that other. In a true dialogue between Gospel and a particular culture it may sometimes be that the word of God is lost or put in danger, but in fact it finds itself more fully. That is to say, the infinite riches of God's communication to humankind which can never be perfectly formulated in human language—not even the language of the Gospel—these infinite riches more adequately manifested as God's word find a newer expression in successive cultures. That genuine dialogue is the key to effective evangelization is implied in the concluding message to the people of God of the synod of bishops in 1977. There is a passage in that message to the people of God where the synod speaks of catechesis—that was the subject of the synod—it speaks of catechesis precisely as ongoing evangelization and it has this very interesting statement:

> Through catechesis the Christian faith must become incarnate in all cultures. A true incarnation of faith through catechesis, supposes not only a process of giving but also of receiving. Here we find one of the precious insights of the second Vatican Council: namely, a better realization that the readiness to receive is a very generous and a very Christian attitude. Traditionally, we have practically identified generosity with giving and we have projected as disloyal the very idea that our church could receive a truth from outside.
>
> After all, it is our Lord himself who according to Saint Paul said that it is more blessed to give than to receive. But the Lord has also taught us by his mortal life the blessedness of receiving, when he emptied himself and accepted the status of a slave, receiving a human nature like ours from his Blessed Mother.

If the Christian faith must, according to the synod, be incarnate in a particular culture it must also in some way empty itself and receive a new human expression. At this point it may be helpful to remember that the perfection of dialogue is not just communication but communion: that is to say, an intimate individual acceptance and caring, and not a mere exchange of information. Today we realize more and more that divine revelation is not only God telling us things, but God establishing a personal relationship with each one of us and manifesting loving concern for us.

Correspondingly, our faith is not so much accepting what God is saying as accepting God himself in our lives, and committing ourselves to God.

This is not to deny the factual content of our creed but to put the accent where it belongs. The give and take of dialogue is particularly important in Asia, because of its highly developed religious and spiritual traditions which are still very much alive today. This appeared with special clarity at the Bishops' Institute for Missionary Apostolate organized by the above-mentioned Federation of Asian Bishops' Conferences in the summer of 1978 in the Philippines.

This Bishops' Institute brought together some twenty prelates from various parts of Asia and about as many priests, religious, and lay people with experiences in various fields of missionary activity. The method that was followed was inductive; that is, the experience of the participants was shared and explored in order to determine what should be the main areas of concern for evangelization in Asia and what the main approach should be to mission in the years to come.

In a concluding statement from the participants it was said:

> From our experience of dialogue emerged the conviction that dialogue was the key to be sought; not dialogue in the superficial sense in which it is often understood, but as a witnessing to Christ in word and deed, by reaching out to people in the concrete reality of their daily lives, in their particular cultural context, their own religious traditions, their social-economic condition.

Besides stressing the importance of dialogue these lines also indicate briefly the main areas in which a fruitful exchange is particularly desirable. First, the insertion of faith in culture; second, the encounter with Asian religions; and third, a certain identity with the condition of so many millions of poor people in Asia. It is very significant and instructive that these same three areas are indicated in a publication put out by SEDOS (a service set up in Rome by superiors general for missionary documentation and study in preparation for the synod of bishops in 1974, which dealt with evangelization). We find that there are three contributions of evangelization in Asia and these three contributions represent three large geographical and cultural areas in Asia, namely the Indian sub-continent, the so-called Far East (mostly Chinese culture), and finally Southeast Asia (Malayan culture).

It is interesting to note that each writer stresses one of the three areas of concern that I mentioned before, while all of them recognize that one is linked with the other. From India comes the statement which says that "an open mind will help us to understand that the Hindu rejection of Christian theology is not necessarily a rejection of Christ; simply that Christ has not been presented in a way that made real sense to the Hindu religious spirit." The conclusion of this writer is "that it is only on the contemplative level that any proper religious dialogue can be engaged in with Hindus."

There is a contribution from Hong Kong, and there the emphasis is on dialogue with culture, though not neglecting also that religious dialogue comes in. And the conclusion of that writer is: "The very way Christianity was proposed seems to have contained an inbuilt incompatibility with the Eastern way of thinking."

And finally there is a reflection from the Philippines bringing out the importance of dialogue with people in their actual economic situation. The conclusion of this writer is: "This then, is the state in which peoples of Southeast Asia are—a state of privation, dependence, and division."

This defines the essential problem of evangelization as the proclamation of the Good News. How to make the Good News really good news to people who are deprived, dependent, divided?

The three-fold challenge that is presented by these writers covers the same three areas that keep emerging whenever the problem of mission in Asia is being discussed. The Bishop's Institute of Missionary Apostolate also developed these three areas in more detail. I will not quote that anymore but I would like to say by way of conclusion that it had not only a strong emphasis on these three areas but also on the fact that the three areas are intimately connected. It is rather easy to see how the dialogue between faith and culture is connected also with religious dialogue; it is perhaps not so easy to see how these two are connected with concern, real concern for the poor, solidarity with the people who are deprived and oppressed. And when that is not affirmed in practice one can have two dangerous positions: one is a kind of archeologism, cultivating the traditions of the past without any concern for the present situation in Asia. And the opposite thing would be that in the name of liberating Asian people, Christians are trying to impose on Asians ideologies which are completely foreign to the Asian spirit.

A balanced and comprehensive approach to mission is what the church in Asia must find and pursue today. There are innumerable problems to be solved and many of them are not peculiar to this continent. What the future has in store is not for us to guess, but there are enough supernatural and natural reasons to go forward with confidence. And in this spirit of confidence we shall conclude with a thought borrowed from the recently published first encyclical of Pope John Paul II. There is in it a section entitled, very appropriately for our purpose, the mystery of Christ as the basis of the church's mission and of Christianity. And in it, the pope speaks precisely of dialogue, recalling that the first encyclical of his predecessor Pope Paul VI was also concerned with dialogue.

This is what Pope John Paul says:

This Second Vatican Council did immense work to form that full and universal awareness of the Church of which Pope Paul VI wrote in his first encyclical. This self-awareness by the church is formed in dialogue, and before this dialogue becomes a conversation, attention must be directed to the other, that is to say, the person with whom we wish to speak. The Ecumenical Council gave a fundamental impulse to forming the church's self-awareness by so adequately and competently presenting to us a view of the terrestrial globe as a map of various religions.

Then he goes on to point out what the Council has said about the great non-Christian religions and the spiritual values enshrined in them. And finally he concluded that particular section with a prayer which I think we can well make our own and with which I shall conclude.

His prayer is that we may consciously join in the great mission of revealing Christ to the world, helping us to find ourselves in Christ and helping the contemporary generations of our brothers and sisters, the people, nations, states, humankind, developing countries, countries of opulence—in short helping everyone to get to know the unsearchable riches of Christ, since these riches are for every individual and are everybody's property.

6

THE CHURCH IN AFRICA

Brian Hearne

When Pope Paul VI visited Kampala some years ago he made the historic announcement to the bishops of Africa, "You may and you must have an African Christianity." Not only "may" but "must." This statement has already had a very profound effect on the church in Africa and it has raised the whole issue of the relationship of the African experience to Christian faith, an issue that has perhaps not received the attention it should have in the past. It was almost a ready-made church that was imported or transplanted from the Western situation into the Asian and Latin American scene, with all the problems that that has raised. The same thing is true of the church in Africa. It is now beginning to respond to the tremendous challenge that was presented to it by Pope Paul VI. More recently still, Cardinal Otunga at the Synod in 1977 said, "We Africans must take ourselves seriously." And by definition, of course, this means that we missionaries must take Africans and the African experience seriously.

The attempts that have been made already to do just this are sketchy and incomplete but I think it is true to say, at least from my vantage point over the past few years, that there is a definite beginning, that there is something new beginning to emerge. To take a couple of examples: we have the creation of the Zaire Mass, an attempt to express in more African imagery and gesture the Eucharistic celebration. In many ways it is not too radical, but at least it's a genuine attempt. An African liturgist from Uganda has often said that the prayers we use in the Mass are far too dry for the African. They need more imagery and specific reference, and you find some of this in the Zaire Mass: the penitential prayer refers to the tick as "the insect that sits on our skin and sucks our blood away, so evil has overcome us, Lord have mercy." This kind of imagery is indicative of a very ordinary, very practical sign of an attempt to think out things anew in relation to the African experience.

Work done by an Irish missionary in Turkhana, Father Tony Barrett, is certainly one of the richest experiences I know. It is a genuine attempt to somehow find the celebratory meaning of the Christian faith in a totally new

Fr. Brian Hearne, C.S.Sp., is professor of pastoral theology at the Gaba Institute, Kenya.

context, and indeed in a context where canon law has not reared its ugly head. There is an attempt to incarnate the church in a meaningful way in a completely different cultural situation. So, these are some attempts of the church to implement what the pope said about having an African Christianity, or attempts to localize. Of course one can also mention the experience of the Ethiopian church.

It is a common feature of intellectual criticism of Christianity in Africa at the moment that it is of course an imperialist importation, and this is leading to growing attention being given to what one may call the precolonial experience of Christianity in Africa. There is indeed a great richness in the Orthodox and Coptic traditions, although again one has to say that the Ethiopian church also needs its Vatican II perhaps, its renewal. However, there is a lot to learn from the authentic way in which Christianity has been expressed in Christian traditions other than Catholic ones.

One can also refer to the way in which certain African values are being seriously studied because in practice this is how Africa is taken seriously. We can discern the seeds of the Word within African culture; we can see how in many ways the mysterious action of God through the Holy Spirit has been at work from the beginning of time and has found expression in the many beautiful values that we as missionaries have to learn from the African situation—the value of harmony in the community, of solidarity, of relationships. The point I want to make is that here we have the key reason why there is so much emphasis on small communities in the church in Africa today.

These values are being interpreted theologically. An example is some work being done by Father Charles Nyamiti, a Tanzanian theologian, who has written about how the mystery of the Trinity can be given a completely new dimension by taking as a starting point the African value of life—the greatest value, Life. God is the totality of life and that life in the African version of the word is always sharing. It always involves sharing. Father Nyamiti applies that also to God. "If God, therefore, is the totality of sharing, then God must be the sharer par excellence." Nyamiti gives a very creative meaning to the doctrine of the Trinity which remains for so many Christians in Africa as well as elsewhere a mere intellectual puzzle.

Again I can highlight the oral tradition of Africa: the use of proverb, the use of imagery to express something of the mystery of the human story, the human story in its search for God. I have pointed to one area where there is something tremendously exciting happening and where it seems to me there is a real challenge to missionaries.

A second point is the killing of Steve Biko and the murder of the archbishop of Kampala, both in the same year. Both were Christians who protested against the growing injustice in two entirely different African contexts, in South Africa and in Uganda. I think this indicates to us that more and more a process of confrontation has to develop if the church is to fulfill its missionary and evangelical action in Africa. More and more the church is becoming aware of its responsibility in society and of the fact that it cannot opt out, that it cannot simply be content with Sunday Christianity.

One of the great problems in Africa, recognized by the bishops, is the split between life and faith: the split between African tradition first of all and faith which is presented in a Western form, but also the split between the ordinary concerns of contemporary Africa and the reality of the Christian church. In Kenya, for example, which is looked on by the West as a model of stability, there is a growing trend by which the rich are becoming richer and the poor poorer.

At the last synod I remember a bishop from Zaire trying to characterize the contribution of the different continents. Latin America was characterized by emphasis on liberation; Asia by emphasis on austerity and contemplation; Europe was characterized by a very serious concern for doctrine; the United States was characterized by concern for secularization; and Africa, he said, seemed to be coming out with one voice on the idea of communion, solidarity. The relationship between the search for communion and the search for justice is a complex one and I think a lot of thought has to be given to that in the church in Africa today. "To avoid easy solutions in the name of reconciliation and then to realize that the final goal is not only justice for all but the reconciliation of all" (Steve Biko).

Third, it may well be said that the greatest single issue in Africa today is the relationship of Christianity to Islam. At the recent meeting of the symposium of African bishops in Nairobi a statement on Islam was issued, which at least opens the way to dialogue. It sees the absolute need for a change in relationship between Christianity and Islam, for the sake of Africa, not just for the sake of the church or of Islam. Here we have an example of how the church is growing to see its role in reference to its being in the world. It is no longer so introspective as before and it is more concerned with the good of society. But just raising the issue of Islam is already raising very serious theological problems; for example, the theology of revelation. Can Christians genuinely meet Muslims as brothers and sisters in faith, in a common search for the mystery that lies behind all human reality, in a common search for universal community? These are some of the questions that must be faced by the church in Africa in the next generation. If they are not faced, one can only fear a dreadful cataclysm, and at the moment one can see signs of this: for example, the slaughter of Muslims in Chad by Christians, and the reprisals that are going on at this moment in Uganda against Muslims. What is the role of the church? Was it not possible for a more Christian approach to Islam to be inculcated in people? How is it that these things have been allowed to happen and have even to some extent been approved? The sense of triumph over Islam when somehow or other Christianity again gets the upper hand; the very negative approach to Christianity when Muslims get the upper hand; the refusal to take the fears and the feelings of Muslims seriously. Here we are confronted with a serious need to examine the whole concept of revelation and the role of the missionary with regard to Islam in contemporary Africa.

A fourth point is an even more recent one. The letter of the council of youth of Taizé, that famous center of work for Christian unity and justice in France, was issued from Mathari Valley in Nairobi on Christmas Eve. Mathari Valley is one of the very poor areas where the deprived of the rich Kenyan society live, or try to live, in squalor. Some monks from Taizé went to live there and are still living there, trying to identify themselves with the poor. They decided that the letter from the council of youth should be issued from there as a call to the whole church. I think that letter reminds us of another dimension of the church's task in Africa today, which is to take far more seriously the need to work for reconciliation among the Christian churches. Vatican II pointed out more than ten years ago that there is a major obstacle to evangelizing in the divisions that exist between the churches and that many of these divisions have been imported, having no historical basis in Africa. For this I think the church must grow in a spirit of repentance. One sign of this would seem to be the fact that in June in Nairobi there will be held for the first time an official attempt at dialogue between Catholic theologians and theologians representing the evangelical churches, which represent approximately 80 percent of the Protestant churches in Africa. Here I think is a sign of something that is beginning to happen. Despite all the difficulties and the pain, there is a serious attempt being made to at least face up to the realities of division and to aim at some kind of better understanding on the road to final reconciliation.

These reflections bring me to a final point which I think is the most important one: trying to assess the movements within the church at the moment in Africa—at least some of them. For this I would like to take just three points in time. A catechetical congress was held in 1973 in Nairobi with more than 120 representatives from seven East African countries, which are grouped under the name AMECEA (the association of bishops of East Africa and now comprising eight countries and more than seventy bishops). This grouping is already a sign of a certain development within the church, that is, the growing of regional churches, possibly leading to a new system of patriarchate in the universal church. So the church of the future will be truly a universal church with a truly African church, a truly Indian church, a truly European church, a truly Latin American church, all bound together in a diversity that is the sign of a great communion. But this is being worked out very slowly and the point I wish to make here is to refer to the emphasis at this catechetical congress. It was an attempt to explore the significance of the general catechetical directory from Rome, issued in 1971: to explore the significance of this for East Africa. As a result of that congress it began to emerge that the clear line to be followed in pastoral ministry was to work for adult Christian community. Therefore the emphasis is on adults—not on children—and on community. This particular approach has developed considerably in East Africa and elsewhere over the last few years, and has led to a complete revision of basic priorities of the pastoral ministry in the work of evangelizing. In 1976 at the AMECEA bishops conference, the bishops formally and officially took the options of working for small communities as the basic pastoral option for our time in East Africa. This has presented a tremendous challenge to the church, because it has in fact effectively questioned the whole system by which pastoral ministry is carried out. There are many problems here. One is that, unlike Latin America, the initial impulse has come from the top. But it does correspond with a growing need being experienced by African Christians to experience their own values of community, harmony, and solidarity in the context of the Christian faith.

At the synod of 1977, almost with one voice, the African bishops emphasized the same basic concern, that somehow or other all the problems of the church in Africa converged in such a way that they all call for the setting up of smaller groupings within the larger ecclesial units, that unless this is done, catechesis will remain superficial and will not touch people at the depths of their being. It is only in the context of small communities that Christians can begin to experience, really, the presence of the living Christ. It is only in the experience of small communities in face to face relationships that Christians can begin to live the mystery of the Blessed Trinity.

Perhaps the major concern that we can point to in the church in Africa is that impulse towards questioning pastoral structures, precisely because it is only in reaching a new approach to pastoral ministry in which everyone is involved—and I need hardly point out that that is a constant theme of Pope Paul VI—that the task of evangelization is the same. The work of catechesis, of passing on the faith, is for everybody, not just for a few special or so-called experts. In this context we have seen what is going on in small communities. I think that this possibly is the most important direction that the church is taking, learning also from the independent churches in Africa, which it was common for Catholics to despise. They speak of those very silly people dancing on the roads and so on, and yet independent churches do have that community value. A church in Ghana called Eden Revival Church started recently and this was one of the things that emerged. A member who had been a Catholic said, "When I was a Catholic, I didn't know who my fellow Catholics were, but now I know all my brothers and sisters and can greet them." Perhaps this is the level at which the church in Africa is going to truly get people involved, truly create living faith, truly lead to an authentic and explosive witness in African society.

PART TWO:
PASTORAL ASPECTS
OF MISSION

7

THE CHURCH, THE ICON OF THE TRINITY

Brian Hearne

I would like to begin with an incident which occurred at a meeting of the Canon Law Society in the United States—a rather safe starting point. A very interesting question became the focus of discussion. The question was concerned with the view of the theology of Vatican II which sees the church as communion—a communion of people, as the body of Christ—a community, true, that is structured ministerially, but that is a community first of all, a communion. In view of that basic insight, how can the legal structures of the church be changed so as to bring the concept and model of the church communion to the very center?

I think it is very easy to show that the structures of the church as we have them by and large are dependent on a different model of the chruch, the model of the church as hierarchy. Take, for example, the decision-making process of the church. Insofar as one can detect, there is very little in the way of authentic participation by the people. Decision-making tends to be done on the top level for everybody else. Now this is a model of society which has diminished in most democratic areas but is still preserved in dictatorships.

I think the Gospel shows very clearly the kind of authority that is exercised in the name of Jesus. The mystery of Christianity is about God coming down among his creatures to wash their feet. That kind of insight has to find structural expression in the church; otherwise, it is only a kind of headtrip, a kind of pious dream. Unless it is concretely embodied in the way that we relate to one another, in the way that authority functions, in the way that decisions are taken, in the way that the church's mission is carried out, it doesn't really exist in reality. So that might be the first question: What in fact is the central model of church that we find in the present ecclesial structures, from the universal church right down to the local priest?

Just reflect for a moment on that. What is the reality? We will come back to this later but first, according to that meeting of the Canon Law Society in the

Fr. Brian Hearne, C.S.Sp., is professor of pastoral theology at the Gaba Institute, Kenya.

United States, there is no doubt that in the present legal system, with the present structuring of the church, the present model is church as hierarchy. You'll find all kinds of ways of noting this. One example that I have often heard at conferences is at the beginning of an address. It will begin with something like "My dear Fathers, Sisters, Brothers, and People of God...." In other words, the expression "people of God" is an updated word for the laity. The whole point is precisely the opposite of that: the church is the people of God and the most important element in the life of each one of us is that we are members of the people of God. So it is quite incorrect to speak of certain people as if they were outside the people of God, though of course that is not the intention in such an address.

It is so easy today to use language that appears modern and fashionable and in tune with the latest slogans, without in any way changing our basic structures and our basic thought patterns. And I think this is a very important point for catechesis, schools, and preaching. We can so easily use words and think that somehow we are updated, that we have come to terms with renewal in the church. All we have done is to put in a new set of words, using words which really don't bespeak any reality. Now I believe, and I am speaking here a bit from my own experience, that when we are talking about small communities there is a very great danger that we can use the word "community" about our parish, but it does not necessarily make any difference in the way we treat that community. It can just be the use of a word. So I have really found, especially in meeting with priests, that the fundamental issue is to accept the truly ecclesial nature of grace, that is to say, the truly communitarian aspect of God's dealings with his people. We cannot speak of a relationship with God on the vertical level, to use the familiar image, without necessarily implying a horizontal relationship with one another.

Now that seems obvious, but has that insight been integrated into our approach to life in the church and church renewal, where in fact the guarantee of our relationship with God is found in our relationship with one another? I could give many examples of this. One would be the notion of prayer as a direct relationship with God, which somehow is different from what we do in liturgy. Now evidently there are two different emphases in private prayer and liturgy, but they should not be seen as in any way opposed. In fact the liturgy of the church is the great expression of what the church is, and it is in the context of liturgy that the church is most truly the church, and that each one of us is most truly a member of the church.

Pope Paul and after him Pope John Paul I and Pope John Paul II have insisted that evangelization is the task of every member of the church. Now that is a splendid statement, and yet look at what the church actually does. To what extent is it remotely true that every Catholic is an instrument and agent of evangelization? I shouldn't ask that question because I don't know the answer very well, I can only get certain impressions. I can certainly say in Africa it is far from being one-fiftieth true. It just doesn't happen like that. So somehow we must come to terms with the fact that there is a basic challenge in practice: that it is not something to talk about, it is not just a theory in theology, it has to do basically with our attitudes, with our practice, with our approach to other people. So there is the point that I think we can start off with: the central model of the church. Are we still centering our activity at the moment on the image of the church as hierarchy or is it something much more fundamental? Do we in practice think of the church as hierarchy or are we really trying to implement the notion of the church as communion?

Here I'd just like to put forth some basic background reflections. I am doing this for two reasons. The first is because we may use a lot of words, we may even have certain convictions, but we need a chance to reflect, to see how profoundly important the notion of communion is to the Christian vocation. And second, it may help us to find or discover a line which can in fact convince other people of the importance of this. I would like very briefly to look at some of the essential doctrines of the church and of our faith.

Bishop Christopher Mwoleka of Tanzania is one of the great protagonists of small Christian communities and has done an enormous amount of work in that area. He has based his whole approach on the doctrine of the Trinity and claims that we approach the mystery of the Trinity from the wrong way round; that we see it as a kind of doctrinal puzzle and as a series of concepts and words that we can somehow communicate to people—you know, three Persons in one nature and so on. This, of course, leaves us cold, it leaves most of us cold anyway. Bishop Mwoleka says, and here I think he is speaking with an authentic African accent, that we will understand the doctrine of the Trinity to the measure we are sharing life together. And that unless we are sharing life together, we cannot understand the Trinity no matter what wonderful intellectual grasp we have of it. The doctrine of the Trinity is about reality; it is about what we are as the image and likeness of God. We are in the image and likeness of God, not of a monolithic god but of a God who is communion, a kind of family, however you describe it. So that if we are not sharing life together at depth, we cannot have an adequate understanding of the Trinity.

Now I think this is a very significant idea indeed, as it brings us back to the notion of practice. So if we are to allow the mystery of the Trinity to be reflected in the life of the church—as the great Orthodox tradition has it, the church is the icon of the Blessed Trinity—it must be in terms of relationship. So we have a very simple question to ask. Is the parish as we know it really an expression, at least as adequate an expression as it can be, of the life of the Trinity in that constant process of giving and receiving which bursts out in the joy of the Spirit? It is that process of endless communication, that process of, as some of the great Fathers punned on the great technical word to describe the Trinity, "dancing together." They imagined the Trinity as a dancing of reality—the one and the many—a plurality coming together in the harmony and beauty of the dance. And this is the model of all relationships in the church.

If you accept the model of church as hierarchy, it becomes very difficult to see the Trinity reflected in that life. Why? Because the model of church as hierarchy is based really on the model of a monolithic god, a monarchical god, an authoritarian figure—the pyramid system, where the one on top dictates everything. The model of the Trinity is—although a pyramid is often used—something like a circle of constant interchange and interaction. And I think that this makes a lot of sense when you see what Vatican II says about the church being a place of dialogue within itself as we are told in *Gaudium et Spes*. It tells us that the church must stand forth as a sign of unity and solidarity in the world and must be a place of dialogue: dialogue first of all within itself in its own life so that *every level* in the life of the church is seen as a process of communication with other levels: the level of theology and practice, the level of Bible studies and charismatic prayer, the level of lay people and priests, the level of religious and the clergy, the level of the bishop and priests—every level you can think of must have some kind of dynamic which is reaching out in dialogue to other levels.

In the parish, is that true? What structures for that kind of communication exist? In the parishes that I would be familiar with from my own experience, maybe there are three in Kenya and one in Uganda with that kind of communication. Often where you do find it, it is going on in spite of the parish church. There is a basic human community that people share but which so often is not facilitated, or literally blessed, by the parish. So just reflecting on the mystery of the Trinity, it is a tremendous challenge to ask what the quality of our relationship is in the life of the parish, in the life of our community, in the life of the church as a whole. Is there an adequate reflection of the mystery of the Trinity or do we in fact give the impression through our lifestyle that we believe in a monarchical autocratic god rather than a God who shares life?

This is obviously a point that could be developed at great length. It can be a tremendously exciting idea, that the God who has revealed himself to us as Trinity has done so because he wants to challenge us to a particular quality of life, a particular style of life, and not because he wants to give us some esoteric information about himself as a kind of special privilege. He has revealed himself as he is, so that we can become like him in our own lives.

Our second reflection is on the path of discipleship in the New Testament: the model of discipleship as a model for the church. Now discipleship, as we see in the New Testament, is a process—a gradual process, a growing process which takes time. It is a kind of catechumenal experience, in which adults seek together to know Jesus. The invitation in John's Gospel, "Come and see," remains of primary importance. A group of people hear that invitation "Come and see," and they investigate. Come and search who I am. And this model of discipleship, which is the model that Jesus himself followed, takes on considerable importance for us in our pastoral ministry.

Here again if we ask a very simple question, we may find some disconcerting answers. How many Christians actually are given the opportunity to go through that process in their lives as adults? At the last synod, some of the African bishops were taken by this idea. They made a suggestion—it wasn't accepted by the synod as a whole, but it was certainly suggested and remains a practical possibility—that every Christian who was baptized as a infant should have to go through a long catechumenate experience as an adult, so that there may be a small group of people who together are seeking to know Jesus. Just another model, if you want, or another approach to a very basic issue; it has the great advantage of being very solidly founded in Scripture.

Let us reflect further on the center of our faith, which is the resurrection of Christ, the risen Christ. The resurrection is not just the coming back to life of a dead man; it is the entry into new life of Jesus of Nazareth in such a way that the man Jesus has now transcended all the limits of time and space and has become the universal man. He has become the one in whom we all have our home. And when St. Paul speaks, as he so often does, with the words "in Christ Jesus," that is exactly what he means. We tend to think too easily of Jesus being in us; really the opposite is the case, we are in him. In his risen body all things are brought together and reconciled, as we are told in Colossians and Ephesians. That vision of the resurrection as a totally new creation has made it possible for human beings to, as it were, move out of themselves into a communion with others in the mystery of the risen Christ. In Christ we have the One who has become the transcultural person, the One who has brought to fulfillment that dynamic in his own life of reaching beyond the limitations of his own culture—when speaking to the Samaritan woman, sitting down at table with the prostitutes and the publicans, rejecting all those conventions and false divisions of society. That is the kind of thrust in the life of Jesus that has come to totality with the resurrection. In him now, the risen Christ, every single human being is able to find a home. And every human culture also. This has great significance for mission.

In Africa there is quite a lot of tension, especially among intellectuals, about the "Pale Christ" of the whites, as he has been called by the founder of a church in Zaire: the Pale Christ of the whites, the watery Christ, the Christ that doesn't make sense to blacks. Now we can say in reply that the risen Christ is black, because all black cultures, all black people have their home in him, with the new creation. And he is black because he called blacks to go beyond their blackness. He is white because he called whites to go beyond their whiteness. He is the one who calls every single human being to go beyond their limitations of egoism, and to reach a stage of integration with all that is true and all that is good.

But the point that I just want to make here is that when we speak of the risen Christ we are necessarily speaking of community. St. Paul says, "You are the Body of Christ," to the Corinthians, and he is not just being pious. He is saying what is to him a sober truth, that the resurrected body of the Lord is the church. We are truly the body of Christ, we are the way in which the mystery of the risen Christ is, as it were, made visible to the world. Therefore, we cannot speak of the resurrection as simply an individual thing. It is necessarily community. We are together in Christ. We are in him, and that must find expression in our lives.

Once again a question arises: Does it? Does the resurrection find adequate expression in our present ecclesial structures? Maybe it does, but maybe it doesn't, and of course we are always open to improvement.

Let us take one other basic issue, the question of sin. Sin, as we have grown used to hearing, is nothing more than fundamental selfishness, and the individual sins that people commit are sins because they are the expression of selfishness. It is not simply the wrong actions that we do that are sins. As Jesus himself puts it in Mark's Gospel, "It is not the things that are outside that can defile, it is what comes from within." It is from the evil heart that selfishness, that greed, that desire to center reality on self arises. So sin is, you might say, the same as selfishness. And it is precisely selfishness that makes community impossible. Therefore we can say that grace, which comes to overcome the power of sin, is essentially directed to others, it is other-centered. Grace is the love of God liberating us from the need to center reality on self. It is the gift of God that frees us, puts us into a new order of relationship.

Even a very brief reflection can show us that we cannot speak of sin or grace, at least in ordinary terms, unless in some way we are speaking of relationships. Again this is a very deep idea in African society. Evil in Africa is to break relationship. And here we certainly have something to learn from that tradition. To bring disharmony into a community, to bring quarrelling, to keep an evil heart—all these are seen as essentially sinful. Let me relate this to the whole question of prejudice. Enda McDonagh points out correctly that we tend to be threatened by others, by the strange or by the unfamiliar, and because we are threatened, we close up. We get a bit twisted in on self. The fact that this is the instinctive reaction in human beings can be traced, I think, to our evolutionary past, the aggressivity of the animals, the need to defend one's territory, so that when one's territory is infringed upon one reacts by aggression. And of course for the human our territory is not just geographicial, our territory is mental and spiritual, our whole world-view. So when someone says something that challenges my worldview, my first reaction will be that territorial one—of rejection, of aggression, of self-defence.

Prejudice is a necessary result of sin in us because prejudice is the way that we can keep a self-centered view of the world; we can somehow fool ourselves into thinking that the world is really centered on self. When I think by my prejudices, I am putting myself in a position of superiority over others. Now that again is a bit abstract, but in a group process what do you find? It is very difficult to keep on listening to others; I am already thinking out what I want to say, I am already arguing against it in my own mind, I am already interpreting what I hear, rather than really listening, so that it is difficult to give full attention to what someone is saying; it becomes very easy to misunderstand. It becomes very easy to refuse genuine dialogue and to end up with two people simply having a monologue with one another.

Now that is a very familiar experience. But I think that theologically here we are talking about sin. That is how sin expresses itself, not just in fighting with people or in fornication and so on, but in that basic attitude which makes it difficult to hear what others are saying, that refusal to be welcoming and to be open. That is very often the work of sin which is within us, selfishness and prejudice. And it is the work of grace to enable us to grow into the listening heart of Christ: that gentleness, that at-homeness, that "welcome." Those of you who have any experience in Africa will certainly have experienced the meaning of that word "welcome." Welcome, you are at home— you should feel at home just as if you were at home. If that kind of attitude can be really communicated in our own relationships, then I think we are talking about grace.

There is another basic theological truth I would like to mention: the sacraments. Nothing could be more evident in our faith and in our religion than the fact that the sacraments are essentially social. Jesus himself, when he chose a sign of his lasting presence among us, chose the form of a communal meal. And that was no accident, though we sometimes think that it was perhaps. It has a very profound symbolism—sitting down to eat and drink with other people, moving out of one's own isolation to share with them, not just to eat food by oneself, but to share with other people, to share the good things of creation, the blessings of God, symbols of God's purpose for all humanity. This expression of sacramental existence is essentially communitarian. And that of course is why St. Paul can say, in words that perhaps we have forgotten, to the Corinthians, "Because you are divided into factions among you it is not the Lord's supper you are celebrating." Why? Because by being divided you are contradicting the very meaning of what you say you are doing: expressing your unity in the bread and wine and the Body and Blood of Christ.

As you know from St. Thomas Aquinas, the final purpose and reality of the Eucharist is the unity of the church. So that the answer to the question, Why do we eat the Body and Blood of Christ in the Eucharist, is not just that we may gain grace for ourselves, it is not just that we may have a personal relationship with Jesus. It is so that we may be one, one with one another in him, in his Body: "Though we are many we become one because we all share in the one bread which is the Body of the Lord."

Baptism is an initiation into the community, it is not simply an individual act of receiving forgiveness. In fact it can be argued that in baptism we receive forgiveness precisely because we are integrated into the mystery of the Body of Christ, which is the church. It is a sacrament of, at once, ecclesial fellowship and of forgiveness, and the two go hand in hand. One could look at all the sacraments in that way. In the sacrament of marriage, human relationship is the sacramental reality; there is nothing in marriage but the relationship between two people who want to commit their lives to one another.

Almost wherever you look you'll find that movement into community, into communion, is part of God's purpose. This is the kind of very basic background that helps us to see that the option of building small communities is not just a kind of pastoral gimmick or stategy. It is truly an attempt to make real for people in their lives the central meaning of God's revelation, so that people can experience it where they are in the here and now of their lives. This can be done in their ordinary relationships and they don't have to go away to discover God. God is there in their midst, Emmanuel, among them. To discern his presence, to discern that Hidden Face of Christ present among people in their day-to-day lives, is really the basic reason for the emphasis on small communities.

8

MISSION TODAY

Walbert Bühlmann

We know that mission today cannot be understood without a short reference to mission yesterday. Since missionaries were sent out from Europe to other continents—Asia, Africa, Latin America four or five centuries ago, they were under European hegemony, European leadership, European predominance. Europe was the center of the world: politically, economically, culturally, and also ecclesiastically. We had the Jus Commission, whereby certain territories in certain continents were entrusted to a missionary society which was fully responsible for those territories. They had the full responsibility for bringing missionaries, bringing money, directing the whole Apostolate.

You may remember that in 1965 the first book was published as a kind of reaction to this by African priests: *Black Priests Are Questioning.* It was the very first expression of the mind of African priests, and of the black priests of the two Americas. In the preface of that book they said, "Till now the missionaries did all for us, without us, and often against us, without willing it; but in fact many of their initiatives were against the African interest." Now we know that situation of European hegemony has come to an end in all the sectors political, economic, ecclesiastical—we know that we're in a New World.

I would like to call to your mind five world events which we have heard about during the past twenty years or so, but which perhaps we have not yet fully understood, especially for their impact in creating a New World. Of course these five events are not isolated. They are the tips of the iceberg, they are expressions of movement—the typical expressions of movements of emancipation of the colonial world from the European world.

The first event is Bandung 1955, convoked by Afro-Asian states, some of which were already independent and others of which had nationalist movements. The goal of this conference was to give a new impetus to the movement of decolonization, and we know it gave that new impetus because in the years since then, we have seen this decolonization process come to an end. So

Fr. Walbert Bühlmann is a Swiss member of the Capuchin Order and a former missionary in Tanzania. At present he is Theology Mission Director for the Capuchins in Rome.

Bandung 1955 was the signal for *political autonomy* or *emancipation* of the world.

After the Second World War when the United Nations was founded, there were fifty-seven founder nations: now we have a hundred and sixty members of the United Nations. That means that there are more than one hundred new nations.

The second event was in Paris in 1956: the first congress of black authors and artists from Africa and the two Americas. This congress in Paris was the epiphany of the black culture. We know that all non-European peoples— Asians, Indians, Chinese, Native Americans—have been very much humiliated by the white presence. But more than the other races this applied to the black races of Africa. We were convinced that Africans had nothing to offer; they were savages, pagans, barbarians. At the First Vatican Council a missionary bishop proposed a prayer to the universal church that God would finally take away the curse of Ham from the black race. Paris 1956 was the signal for *cultural emancipation,* and we know now that Africans no longer feel ashamed for being black. They say now that black is beautiful.

The third event was Kyoto 1970: the first congress of world religions for justice and peace in the world. Three hundred representatives of ten different religions came together—Christians altogether were only one of the ten. The Christians no longer presided; they were allowed to talk but all were sitting at a round table. No more dominance by the Christians; all took each other very seriously. So Kyoto 1970 was a signal for the *religious emancipation* of the world.

Then we have Algiers 1973—an economic congress of African-Asian states. In that congress members said: we are still dominated by Western economy, by world trade. The price of our raw materials is fixed in London, in Manhattan, in Paris. Yet, if we keep together we can break this dictatorship of world trade. And some few months later the world got its first experience of the oil crisis. Algiers 1973 was the signal for the *economic emancipation* of the Third World.

Finally we have Rome 1974, the episcopal synod on evangelization. We can say, of course, that this movement of emancipation began in the Vatican Council. You will remember that the First Vatican Council spoke of the one church, the Roman church, the central power, the infallibility of the church, of the pope, in a word the one central power of Rome as the model for all churches. The Second Vatican Council, completing the teaching of the one church, spoke also of many churches, the local churches, the episcopal power. So now we have two powers in the church: we have the central power in Rome and the power of the bishops in the many local churches. These two powers have to be in dialogue with each other and create an equilibrium: not only giving in but keeping up their own interest in real dialogue and building up the many churches in unity.

Since the Council of Trent and the First Vatican Council, the key words in the Catholic church were unity and uniformity. In liturgy, in theology, in all the catechisms, in all of our translations of European catechisms this was applied. In the Second Vatican Council for the first time the bishops spoke of pluriformity. They did it very prudently, very cautiously, in terms of a desire to accept, to receive this pluriformity. Ten years later in 1974, the African bishops spoke very clearly of the rightness of the Africanization of Christianity. They said, "Till now we Christianized Africa, but now we have to Africanize Christianity." And the ideas of these African, Asian, and Latin American bishops entered *Evangelii Nuntiandi,* and now in *Evangelii Nuntiandi* pluriformity is no longer just admitted as a right but is required as a duty.

In *Evangelii Nuntiandi* (Nos. 30 and 63), there is a very clear sentence which says that local churches have the duty, not the right but the duty, to translate the message of the Gospel into their own languages and, the pope adds, not only literal languages, but cultural languages, translated into their own culture so that the Gospel, incarnated in the new culture, will be understood by the people. He said this has to be done in the fields of theology, of liturgy, of catechesis, and of secondary church structures. So we have the many local churches in unity through pluriformity. I think that Rome 1974 was a turning point for the whole church. It was the signal for *ecclesiastical emancipation,* in the good understanding of the word, though we always retain the concept of the one Catholic church.

I would say that the synod of 1974 was the summit of the pontificate of Paul VI, and the whole pontificate of Paul VI was, for me, a turning point in church history. I think Paul VI entered church history as that pope under whose pontificate the Western church has become a world church: a church of six continents. In his time, in the fifteen years of his pontificate, the center of gravity which was always in the Western world (and at the beginning of this century 85 percent of all Christians were still living in the Western world) has shifted, because now the majority of Christians are living in the southern hemisphere. They are now in Latin America, Africa, and Asia, and this trend will continue in the future. We can foresee that in twenty years time 70 percent of Catholics will be living in the southern hemisphere.

So the pope systematically appointed local bishops. In Africa, of the three hundred and fifty bishops roughly 75 percent are Africans. In Asia, practically 100 percent of the bishops are Asians. Twenty years ago, when Pope John XXIII was elected, Africa had not yet any cardinal; Asia had two. In the recent conclaves Africa had twelve cardinals; Asia-Oceania also had twelve. Another fact: we can say that since the first pope, Peter, came to Rome, no pope had ever left Europe until this pontificate. The pope lived and travelled only in Europe; by travelling abroad he declared that the church has become a church of six continents. Thus you can see that the summit of his pontificate was the synod of 1974. It was a real turning point. The Second Vatican Council and the first three synods were still managed by the Western bishops and Western theologians: this synod of 1974 for the first time was clearly managed by the bishops and the theologians of the Third World. They proposed the important ideas which entered *Evangelii Nuntiandi,* and so the

Third Church for me is not only the church of the Third World, but at the same time, the church of the coming third millennium.

The first millennium was under the leadership of the First Church, the Oriental church which began in the center with the first eight councils, all in the East. The second millennium was under the leadership of the Second Church, the Western church—our church which was built up in the Middle Ages and which undertook all the missionary work of the past five hundred years. Now the coming millennium will, according to my conviction, be under the leadership of the Third Church. It began at the synod of 1974 and I am convinced that the great ideas and inspirations for the future will come for the whole church from Latin America, Africa, Asia. Therefore we see that we are, in contrast to the last five hundred years, living now in an emancipated world and in an emancipated church.

As we have CELAM for Latin America and an episcopal conference for Africa and for Asia we also have an episcopal union for Europe. And I know they are preparing a document on their self-identity, explaining their standard and their function in Europe. They will have to declare how they feel now about the church. In the past they failed to be the church. Now they feel they have become a part of a bigger church, a church of six continents. Now in the new situation, we need new mentalities, and we can reduce these new mentalities to one mentality—that we have to go from European and Roman monologue to dialogue.

First, we must dialogue with other religions. In the past we had no dialogue with other religions. We tried to get converts, to take people out of their religions, to convert them into the church. We spoke on the religions, against the religions, but not with the religions, and in spite of all our mission effort we know that two-thirds of humanity are still not Christians. We no longer call them pagans. For the past fifteen years we have called them other religions: Buddhist and Hindu and so on. More and more we realize now that they are partners, our partners on their way to God. That the spirit of Christ is already working in the midst of these religions and on the basis of this new interpretation, we have, since the Vatican Council, begun a dialogue with the religions. What has happened in the last fifteen years in Asia is for me a tremendous experience. I would say it is more important than the four hundred years of missionary effort in Asia.

The missionary effort in Asia was very small yet it was enough to create local churches, minority and local churches, and now these small, very small, local churches are in a position to organize this dialogue with the religions. They also bring the religions into a dialogue among themselves so the small Christian churches in Asia are very powerful churches, in the sense of opening this dialogue.

We have to dialogue with our catechumens and Christians. In the past missionary schools, we had the mission stations as a state within the state, it was helpful to be a Christian. We provided from birth all that our Christians needed. This time has also come to a marked end. In most countries the schools are nationalized. All countries have independence and many Christians now apply independence also to the church. They feel much more independent, much more free towards the missionary or the local priests. And so we no longer have the old power of the Christians, we have only an immortal power of dialogue. We can use the method of basic communities, which is stressed very much in Africa and in Latin America.

We have to open the dialogue now with the local churches. In the past we said that mission activity had as its main goal to implant the church, to create the church and to build up the local churches. That was in theory and in practice the first goal of missionary activity. Now, as we can see, the local churches are built up. They are founded and it is very clear that they are still young churches in need of help, but yet they are local churches. Most bishops are local bishops and so it is with priests, sisters, and Christian communities. We no longer need to insist on creating or founding local churches but on collaborating with the local churches. We have progressed to a new theological thinking. We have to accept the so-called euthanasia of missionaries, of the missions. We have to prepare the way for the local churches and then we have to diminish, to disappear even, if necessary. It requires a very strong psychological conversion to go back in the second rank, to be no more the strong founder, the strong figure, but to be in the service of the local churches.

This collaboration is done in terms of finances, but not as in the past when we simply gave money, as much as possible. Today all money has to be directed towards the goal of self-reliance, of self-sufficiency, and all investment of money has to be done in view of preparing the foundation of a self-sufficient local church. On the other hand, investments have to be directed, have to develop in a country so that there is no longer dependence on church structures, but in such a way that people become better off and able to maintain their church themselves.

The collaboration of personnel is also still needed at different levels. In our Capuchin Order I would say we have actually three very different situations. We have been in northern India for one hundred and fifty years. At the end of the Second World War we had nine dioceses with nine Capuchin bishops and Capuchin missionaries from several countries. Since then all these dioceses have gone into the hands of local clergy, local bishops, local sisters. There are small groups of Capuchins left. For instance, out of a large group from the Paris province who had been there for over a hundred years, there are now three fathers left, all of them between seventy-five and eighty years old. They know very clearly that they are the last representatives of their tribe. They will die out in a few years and the missionary era will be finished; it is the same way in all the other nine dioceses.

In Tanzania, on the contrary, we have a typical case of transition. There the local clergy is as strong as the foreign missionaries. The local sisters are much more numerous than the foreign sisters. Christians are increasing. Once we had about one hundred Swiss missionaries there; now we give over one or two parishes to the local clergy each year and the missionaries are retiring, going back to Switzerland. Young missionaries are spreading out to different dioceses of Tanzania to work there, collaborating in small groups in one or two parishes. Where we see our mission is finished, we are still collaborating in the service of the local churches as far as we are needed.

A third case is Chad, for instance, in central Africa, where there are very recent missions, only twenty or thirty years old. The local clergy are very few—two, three, or four in a very big region—and there we see we are still needed for twenty years or more. So it depends very much on the situation, but as a whole we can say our mission, that means the mission done by foreign missionaries, is declining or is coming to an end. The mission done by local clergy, religious, and Christians is increasing.

So I dare to say that the missionary institutes have fulfilled their historical task. They were founded about a hundred years ago for going into the missions on their own initiative because at that time there were not yet churches to dialogue with them. They didn't even ask, do you want us or not? They simply went in the name of Christ. This situation has changed; we have built up local churches, we are now in dialogue, we have no longer a monopoly as missionary institutes. Besides the missionary institutes, we now have the local dioceses of Ireland, of Germany, of France, sending secular priests in groups and forming a kind of partnership with another diocese. This is very normal; we never will have a missionary monopoly. These new efforts by dioceses are not seen as competition but as very good complementary action.

Today we also have many lay movements. Ten years ago some of them humbly asked different mission institutes, do you need us, can we help you, can you accept us as lay missionaries? Today they do not ask any longer. They know and they are convinced that they are missionaries. They have the right and the duty to go out as missionaries, they do it, and they do it very well. Even when they return after three or five years they go on being missionaries in the different towns of England and of France and so on.

But, especially, we no longer have a monopoly because now the local churches are in control of our missionary churches. *Ad Gentes* (No. 20) explained the very new idea at that time. Twenty years ago in the Vatican Council they stated that the young local churches are a copy of the universal church, a part of the universal church, and all have to be missionary churches by nature. In the past we were convinced that we missionaries were missionary churches, but now all the churches are so, and now in many countries like Tanzania, India, and other countries there are national missionary institutes.

We have lay people doing missionary work. In the past we always had catechists but catechists paid by the bishop, by the parish priest; that means we had a monarchical, organized missionary system: the bishop, the parish priest, and the catechist as the long arm of the missionary. Today, we have a spontaneous expansion of the church, and the basic communities and all the real Christians in Latin America, Africa, and Asia are doing missionary

work. I could tell you many experiences I have had in the last few years in
various countries in Africa. Take one case in Mozambique. I was there just a
few months after independence. For some years the local missionaries had
been building up the local communities. First they also had the system of
bishop, parish priest, and catechists paid by the parish priest, but they said
this system had no future and they prepared groups in the communities to
take responsibility for different ministries, for the different tasks and functions in the community. In one station, for instance, there were twelve
thousand Catholics in the countryside in fifty outstations. I read the statistics
they had presented the year before: six hundred baptisms of children and
seven hundred baptisms of adults. The parish priest told me that seven hundred adult catechumens had been brought to the church by the Christians.
The Sunday service is two hours or more of singing, of praying, and of reading the Gospel. The people are so happy that when they go home they tell their
friends and relatives who are not yet Christians to come and see how they
pray, and they come from curiosity or because Africans are a spiritual people
and they understand. They listen and they say, that is good, and they come
again, and then they become catechumens and after two or three years, they
are baptized.

So you see it is a spontaneous expansion of Christianity. All the churches
have become missionary churches in the active sense. If we speak of missionary crisis, and we are right in speaking of missionary crisis, we should see
it as a typical Western phenomenon. We are in a missionary crisis, we have a
lack of vocations, we have doubts of faith. We ask why still missions? Are
missions still needed since people can be saved in other religions? At the same
time I would say that the missionary crisis in our church was necessary, that it
was providential. If we still had as many vocations as we had twenty years
ago, and each institute sent out fifty more missionaries and fifty more sisters,
the local church would say, please keep away, we don't need you any more in
this country. They still need some help—sisters, fathers, and lay people—but
no longer in large numbers as they did in the good old days.

The missionary crisis was necessary to bring to an end the monopoly which
we had for some hundreds of years when only we sent missionaries. Now we
have to bring this monopoly to an end so that the local churches have room to
grow and to accept the challenge to be missionary churches in their own right.

The last question now is the future of the missionary institutes. If they have
fulfilled their historical task, what is the future of the mission institutes? I
would say they have still a task for a long time, to collaborate financially and
with personnel. They no longer have the responsibility for the missions but
rather the responsibility of performing a kind of inter-ecclesiastical service, a
service between the churches. The second task of these mission institutes is to
be the missionary conscience of the church, of the old churches, which support them, and of the young churches, where they are working. The reason is
that all churches have the temptation to be only a local church, to be satisfied
with the group of Christians they already have. Missionary effort always

needs a new impetus, a new eruption of the Holy Spirit or a new assistance of classical missionaries. So in our old churches, we have to be this mission conscience that our Christians, our bishops, our priests, be always open to this missionary outlook to the whole church. In the young churches we have to bring this missionary dynamic so that these young churches really become missionary churches.

In this context also, the classical missionaries, the foreign missionaries, have to be ambassadors between the churches. They must bring the values and experiences of our churches to the other churches and bring back from those churches their pastoral experiences as a kind of reverse mission. In the past, as you know, we had the one-way system: we had all and we gave a little of our richness. Today, all churches have to give something but also need to receive something from the other churches.

The third task of these mission institutes is to discover new missionary tasks. Perhaps it will be in countries where there are not yet local churches— there are some countries like China which may be open soon again—but especially to discover missionary tasks in our situation, in our own country. All the countries of Europe, of North America, are mission countries again today. Maybe this is exaggerated but in all those countries there are mission situations. In France, around Paris, 3 to 5 percent of the people still go to the churches. Italy alone has about sixty thousand priests, which is two times more than Latin America, four times more than the whole of Africa. The sixty thousand priests in Italy are occupied with 30 percent of the Italian population, the 30 percent who more or less come to the churches. In the United States they speak of eighty million un-churched people. In black Africa, for eighty million people there are five thousand priests and ten thousand sisters. In the United States, for these eighty million un-churched people, there are very few priests or sisters or lay people who systematically try to contact the eighty million un-churched people. Mission institutes have to discover this new situation. Since *Evangelii Nuntiandi* we no longer divide the church into missionary countries and non-missionary countries. The pope no longer divides territories, but he distinguishes classes of people: those who are not yet Christians, the Christians, and those who no longer are Christians. For the "not yet Christians" and the "no longer Christians," who are really outside the church, the church has the priority task of bringing them the Gospel, to give them a first proclamation of the Gospel.

Today it is no longer possible or necessary to repeat simply what our founders a hundred years ago wanted to do. We have to ask ourselves what would our founder, our foundress do if he or she lived today. This is the new task which we have to discover and implement. So we see that the situation in the world and in the church has radically changed, but human beings remain essentially the same. Their longing for a lasting answer to the search for sense in their lives, their longing for hope and for salvation mean that evangelization is necessary. So the church as a whole and we, as members of the church, always have this task and this mission of bringing evangelization and hope and salvation to the whole of humankind.

9

DIALOGUE WITH OTHER RELIGIONS

Parmananda Divarkar

In Asia, and certainly in east Asia, dialogue is regarded more and more as *the* area of concern today and precisely of concern for the missionary, for the evangelizer. First of all, it is no longer regarded as either a substitute for evangelization or a preliminary, but more and more it is being regarded as evangelization itself and, in the concrete situation of Asia, the best form of evangelization, of getting the message of Christ across to our brothers and sisters in Asia. At one time it was regarded, as I said, at best as an introduction, as pre-evangelization; at worst as a substitute—when we couldn't do anything better. I am not going to enter that discussion. I merely say that more and more it is being regarded as *the* area to be cultivated and to be concerned about.

The second point is that it is being felt more and more that the dialogue is not just a concern in Asia of missionaries and evangelization but that, if we succeed in making a breakthrough in that area, it could mean something tremendous for the church as a whole. It would really be a breakthrough into the new era of the church in which we might not even recognize the church as we have known it.

The third thing I would say is that although a lot of reflection, exchange of experiences, and research has been made in this area recently, and there has been a lot of progress, it is felt that there is still a vast area to be covered. So I am not being modest when I say that I can't do justice to the subject. In a sense I don't think anybody can do justice to it because we are still finding our way.

I begin by recalling some simple psychological insights into this whole question of dialogue, interpersonal dialogue and relations, which I think are very relevant to religious dialogue and eventually to religion itself because religion is a dialogue with God.

I speak first of communication and communion, because dialogue is com-

Fr. Parmananda Divarkar is a Jesuit priest from India and a member of the General Superiors Council in Rome.

munication and religion is communion with God. The classical analysis of communication shows two fundamental elements in its content and expression. In our seminaries when we were learning how to preach, they were the two things that were stressed. You must have something to say; you must know how to say it and get it across. Arrangement was part of expression—not say the nasty things first, to work your way into the hearts of people, and so on. Today it is being seen that there is a third element which does not really go in line with the other two but is much more fundamental, and that is mutual acceptance between the people who are communicating. It sounds so obvious that it could be left out. If you don't want to listen to what I'm saying or I don't want to talk to you, obviously there is going to be no communication. What is being realized is how much that acceptance is part of communication; you understand things to the extent that you are really open to listening. Listening is not just hearing—it means much more. The minimum would be just giving the person the benefit of the doubt or being ready to put up with that person and when we speak of personal communication, and not just the communication of information, this mutual acceptance is just about everything. When there is real personal communication, when it becomes communion, you can almost dispense with content and expression. The more intimate two people are, the less they need to express their intimacy; it exists by itself. The content is the intimacy itself. There can also be other content but basically what they are enjoying is not the exchange of information; it is the intimacy itself. So that mutual acceptance becomes content, becomes expression.

All the same, it is obvious that at least to start this bond of intimate dialogue one needs some expression; the same is true for keeping it going. These are obvious things but they have some relevance to what I am going to say a little later. It is also realized that although content and expression—communication in the more obvious sense of the word— help intimacy, they can also come in the way of intimacy. They can be made a substitute for intimacy. When you meet someone, the less intimate you are the more need there is to keep something happening all the time, otherwise it becomes embarrassing to lapse into silence. So this expression is really a substitute for intimacy. It can be a positive defense against intimacy. As long as something is happening—a cup of tea is being stirred—nothing intimate is going to happen.

This intimacy, this personal relationship, this mutual acceptance, in a way colors content and expression. Not only do you understand a person better when you are on the same wave-length, but, in a true sense, what that person is saying acquires a new meaning. A very banal example: if a friend says that his or her birthday is April 24, that date acquires a new meaning, it becomes operative in your life. So this mutual acceptance, intimacy, is real communication at the personal level. Content and expression to some extent serve that intimacy but they can also get in the way, can be an obstacle.

At this level of content and expression one can, sometimes unconsciously, manipulate. At the level of pure intimacy you are, so to say, helpless, defenseless, vulnerable. Content and expression can in many subtle ways, in many obvious ways also, be manipulated. You can move into your own ground and the other person is at a disadvantage. You ask all the questions, the other person is on the defensive. So that area lends itself to manipulation. At that deeper level of real intimacy both are exposed in a sense, both are vulnerable. But that's where a real creative relationship can take place. So obviously, real dialogue, personal dialogue, should be at the level of intimacy, of togetherness, of mutual acceptance.

There was a time, not so very long ago, when on principle there was no mutual acceptance. It was felt to be a betrayal, a disloyalty. And therefore, there was no real dialogue. There was debate if you like, controversy, trying to prove the other wrong—but no mutual acceptance. Incidentally, mutual acceptance does not necessarily mean approval. You can accept a person without approving of what he or she says or all that he or she stands for. That's what most people want, to be accepted simply, basically, as persons. Later, and this was still pre-Vatican II, there was acceptance, there was good will, but the dialogue was carried out entirely at the level of content and expression: What does your religion teach? Why does it teach that? How does it get this across? There was dialogue, but at a rather superficial level. The progress that has been made today is to have religious dialogue at the deeper level; the current word for this is the level of religious experience. I don't want to hear about your ideas or what your religion has to say about this; I just want to know how you experience God. What is it that makes you feel that somehow there is a power beyond? Or that you are accepted by God? It is at that level that dialogue has been found to be extremely fruitful.

Obviously, our experience is conditioned by our ideas. Two people may have the same experience, but they interpret it in the light of their ideas. To that extent, even in sharing religious experience, you have to explain yourself, but the explanation takes a very secondary place and it comes in an atmosphere of mutual acceptance. If I accept your idea of God and you say, "Well, for me, God is an impersonal being," I can accept it in the sense that I accept you and your experience. It doesn't mean that I approve of that idea. But it is a nonjudgmental acceptance, which could not be made at the other level where we were asking, is there such a thing as an impersonal God? But we are not talking about that. You are saying that you experience God as an impersonal being. I can't question that, if that's the way you experience God. It is a fact and I accept that fact that you experience God that way. Of course, this dialogue is not between religions, it is between people who are religious who claim to have some experience of God, some concern for God. Religions cannot dialogue in this sense.

There is a lot of this dialogue happening. I can only speak for India. I have taken part in it, mostly with Hindus and to some extent with Muslims and many other smaller groups. The main thing is that this was at the level of religious experience.

Our traditional understanding of religion has followed more or less the pattern of going from something more external, tangible, and sensible, to something deeper. The classical, traditional analysis of religion which used to be found in books divided it into religion, code, and cult: a set or system of public, common worship. Fairly early, around the turn of the century, it was realized that this was only the crust of religion—there is something at the heart which was left out. I don't remember the exact terms used by Baron Von Hugel, for example, but the first one was certainly mystical. By mystical he meant what today we would call experiential—the experienced level of religion. I think the second term used was the rational or the intellectual level, conceptualizing experience. To make it intelligible to yourself you have to reflect on it and try to formulate it somehow. Finally he called it institutional or social—the structural, the external communitarian aspect of religion which in a way included all three: creed, code, and cult. The creed of course came a little bit into the rational element also, but the main thing was the introduction of this mystical or experiential element as being at the heart of religion; everything else was a development. The experiential element is, in our relationship with God, the same as mutual acceptance, while creed, code, and cult are like content and expression. They correspond at least, even though they may not be exactly the same thing.

Today I think we have gone one step further though at first sight it is like taking a step back rather than a step forward. Some are saying that, in fact, religion is just creed, code, and cult. There is something else but it is something that is not religion; it is something deeper than religion. If you like, this is a matter of words. In our terminology some would use the words "faith" and "religion" and make a distinction between them. They would say that faith is what many people think religion is but, in fact, religion is external and faith is contact with God, experience of God. They would make a sharper distinction between this mystical element I spoke of before and wouldn't put it simply in line with the other two. They would say the mystical, rational, and institutional don't come in a line. The mystical, the experiential, is a world apart and is really the heart of our relationship with God. The other two should be put separately; they shouldn't be put in a series.

In order to make that distinction they would call the first dimension faith—personal relationship with God—and everything else would be religion. After all, Our Lord himself says, "Eternal life is to know the one true God"; not to *know about* God, not to *do* something about God, but to have a *personal relationship* with God, to know God. It is interesting that when talking about personal relationships we always us the term "to know": I know someone. And yet it is a very special kind of knowledge. It is not the same as knowing about someone. It cannot be itemized. And yet it is knowledge. So the mutual acceptance we spoke about is knowledge and yet is not information. And eternal life is to know God, is to have that relationship with God.

What is being said today is that the really divine element in religion—in the Christian religion, for example—is that level of faith: knowing God and being known by God, being called by name by God. Everything else is, to a greater or lesser extent, a human effort to live that experience, to give expression to that experience, to find somehow a context in which that experience can be fostered, can grow. But even many Catholic theologians would say that at this secondary level we can admire a lot that is really human. It could be purely human in the sense of having been invented by human beings—even in the Catholic religion—it could be human in the sense that it was suggested by Christ. In other words, the whole thing becomes relativized in terms of that basic experience and it loses a certain amount of its importance. It is important only in terms of that basic faith. Moreover, they will say, just as I said about communication, this other level can help but it can also be a hindrance. It can be made a substitute for praying. You think you are manipulating God as if by some superstition: if you have done this, then God is somehow committed to doing something for you. We can defend ourselves against God by praying, keep God at a certain distance (if I am saying my prayers, God is at the other end but I know that if I stop saying my prayers, God will come too close and I will feel threatened). These are ways in which one can misuse communication and make it an obstacle to communion and this can apply also to religion. Communication can become an obstacle to communion.

Let us take something a little more concrete. These two elements—the deeper one, communion with God, and the more external one, creed, code, and cult—are found in every religion. Formerly we tried to distinguish between false and true, natural and supernatural. There is a certain supernatural element in every religion because God has called every person; God wants everyone to be saved and to come to the knowledge of the truth. So everyone has the possibility of personal contact with God.

Another thing that enters very much into this question of dialogue with other religions is that although all religions have these two elements—I speak of the so-called great religions as opposed to tribal religions which are very localized—all of them have grown either in West Asia or in East Asia. West Asian religions are Hinduism, Buddhism, Confucianism. Broadly speaking, the West Asian religions are historical in that they are tied up with the history of a particular people. Not only do they have historical founders and figures but they were also, from the very beginning, community religions, state religions, if you like. The East Asian religions are non-historical; some of them have no known founder, though that's not the important thing. In none of them does the founder really enter into the religion. Besides that they are unconcerned with the course of history; they are much more a-cosmic.

In the historical religions there is a tendency to put the accent on creed, code, cult. Not that the other is ignored by any means. But, inevitably, by the very way the religion has grown and developed, the accent is strongly on the creed, code, and cult. In the East Asian religions, which are a-historical, a-cosmic, the accent is put on this deeper dimension, understood in all kinds of ways. I'm not trying to justify that, but definitely there is a tendency to relativize creed, code, and cult in relation to this deeper experience of God understood differently in different religions. That, I think, is an important point to notice.

I think that Our Lord in his whole message was trying to put the accent on faith, on knowing God: that is eternal life. So much of his effort was precisely to relativize the laws and structures: worship in spirit and in truth is not done either on this mount or that mount. Christianity in its spirit—though it is rather crude to try to put it in these categories—really belongs to the other tradition of putting the accent on faith, on contact with God, on worship in spirit and in truth. But historically and concretely it belongs to the West Asian tradition; its continuity with Judaism leaves no doubt at all about that.

Because of that weight of history and because we are human beings we tend constantly to shift the accent to creed, code, and cult. It is much more comfortable to handle God if we have a creed, code, and cult. We can manipulate God and so it is a constant temptation. So these are two traditions, two ways in which God has, on his side so to speak, reached out to humanity. Neither of the ways is exclusive but there has been a historical dispensation which developed in East Asia. Christianity is really the fulfilment of both these traditions. Christ is really the fulfilment of both—he brings them to perfection.

The Christian missionary has tried to dialogue or to judge or to contact or to reach out to these East Asian religions in the framework of creed, code, and cult. Some have put it very simply. You treat Hinduism as if it were a church, you judge it as if it were a church. However, not only the word "church" but also anything related to church structures has absolutely no meaning in Hinduism. So you find fault with it because it doesn't supply answers and it seems to be shifting its ground all the time. What are your beliefs? We don't have a creed. Then how can you be a religion if you don't have a creed? And we don't have a code, we don't even have a cult. So how can you be a religion at all?

Ultimately Christian missionaries were being unfair to themselves. To relate religiously at the level of creed, code, and cult is unfair on both sides. That's the tragedy—both sides have been losing. So now the idea is to try to relate at that deeper level and to realize to what extent these other elements—creed, code, and cult—can be relativized. We are beginning to realize more and more that there is much more room for relativizing these things than we thought.

10

RECOGNIZING OUR GOD

Priscilla Sequeira

Christian witness in our world today is to be, as in the past, a witness to God. But it is not so simple. We are witnesses of ourselves, witnesses of culture, our tradition, our past. As a Western people, we have a past, we have traditions, and we are conscious of our traditions.

It is not so easy to distinguish between being a witness to God and being a witness to our Western culture, our Western past. Neither is it easy to be witnesses to the true God because there are so many gods in our world, just as in the past there were many false gods. That is the reality we are facing every day in Latin America.

The problem is, who is God? Where is God to be found? We are in a struggle between the true God and the false gods. The true God is very different from the others. The first characteristic is that Our Lord is always of the future. We never know our God completely and perfectly. We know what he did in the past; we do not know what he is doing right now and what he is going to do in the future. That is his message: a new reality. Our God is to be discovered by ourselves, to be revealed to ourselves. Our Christian witness is different from that of the old priests, the holders of sacred documents in the present. Today there are many holders of established theologies, established ideologies, who consider themselves owners of God, because they are the owners of the right doctrine about God. We are witnesses to God but we are not owners of God.

For priests, for religious people, it is very difficult not to consider ourselves as the owners of God. Occasionally we hear that we give the impression of being in the world like owners, proprietors of God. We know about God. According to the Christian message we are holders of the old traditions, the past actions of God, but God is not only acting in the past. All God's actions in the past have to be new in our world so that we are witnesses of the actions of God in our world. All the actions in the past are symbols, traditions, orientations, in order to understand what God is doing now in our world. Before announcing, before explaining, we have to discover our God. Where is he

Priscilla Sequeira is a journalist from São Paulo, Brazil.

acting? Where is he active, effective in our world? What is he saying, revealing, in our world today? Our mission is one of witness, of seeking in our world where God is present.

Our mission is not to show to the others the God that is our property. It is showing the God who is acting in our world. And from a Latin American church viewpoint, this is very important. The traditional church was just like an owner. And because the higher class, the dominating owners of the world, spoke about a God they could not discover, they could not see the reality of God's action. As Christians we are witnesses of the action of God now in our world today because our God is acting in our society. That is another difference between the false gods and the true God. Our Lord is changing, transforming human society.

That is the God from the Bible, different from the others, different from the ideologies of our world. Our God does not accept the human world and human society as it is. He is entering into our world for a struggle. Our whole beautiful history reveals a God struggling. A permanent conflict between God and false gods: that is his action. God is acting in human society in order to denounce and destroy the false gods and to establish the kingdom. As witnesses we have to discern between the false kingdoms of the false gods and the true kingdom of the true God.

God is acting but not in the same way all over the world. Our God has preferences and priorities, particular ways. This is the difficulty. God is not equally present in the world in all persons, in all circumstances. He has priorities; we recognize them from the Bible. What are the priorities? The election of Israel is a sign, the whole of history is a sign, of a pre-election, a preference in God's action. The first priority is the poor.

In poor and oppressed people God acts. In the first place he enters into this world through the poor, the oppressed, the rejected, marginalized people. That is so clear in biblical history and so clear after that, in the whole of Christian history.

Among poor people all over the world God really acts and develops the kingdom. To discover this we have to travel, we have to discover the world, the other person. God is always acting in the other person we are ignoring, the other person we never considered, never contemplated. In the person totally rejected by society, there is God: active, and active for the kingdom.

In Latin America a clear perception of the church, as seen from the episcopal conferences in Medellín and Puebla, is that God is really creating something new, that God is really founding the kingdom, but not among the powerful persons in this world. God is founding the kingdom among the poor people, the rejected people, those totally abandoned, marginalized by the forces of our world of today.

One of the biggest problems of the church is that very often Christians tend to be witnesses to their ideas, witnesses to doctrines, witnesses to Christian ideologies, but not witnesses to the action of God, to God's reality in our world today. The mission of Christianity is the announcement and demonstration of the reality of God's action in our world today. All over the world, the special place where god is acting is among the poor. He is not creating a new church, but he is creating a renewal, a revival of the church. According to Paul's apostles the church is to be renewed by new communities who are able to transform the old communities. Only by transformation of the old communities will Christians receive from others new expressions of God's action in this world. We in Latin America are witnesses of God's action among the poor, a concrete reality.

Our God is weak compared with the financial power of Wall Street. Compared with the power of the church, he is weak. But he is strong because he is able to create a new kingdom among poor people who have nothing, whose problems every day include food and survival and other immediate material problems. Among them God is able to create a new kingdom and extraordinary faith, extraordinary solidarity, extraordinary hope: a hope we in the Western countries do not have. We have such beautiful speeches, beautiful considerate words, beautiful theologies. But it is the real faith and hope in God that counts. God is powerful to be able to create among the poor belief in him. And that is the testament we are witnesses to in the world.

If we consider the economic, political, and military world, God seems to be absent; people from the Western countries have the impression that God is dead. God really is absent in the banks, factories, the enterprises, the big corporations. But God is acting in Jesus Christ and he is really present there. The spirit is efficient; God is creating a new kingdom among the poor from whom we expect nothing. Our God is extraordinary: different from the realities of this world, totally indifferent to economic and political powers, very different from other gods and also different from the god of the dominating classes, the god of the aristocracies. We are witnesses to the true God acting in our world. We are witnesses, collaborators of the unique witness. Finally there is only one witness as is said in the revelation of St. John: "There is only one witness, Jesus Christ." We are only the servants of this witness, the servants of the testimony of Jesus Christ. We are witnesses to liberation because God is creating a real liberation. We cannot know the final end or aim of that liberation, but there is a process in liberation, going on in our world today. That is the story of the conversion of the old church, the primitive church. The first Christian communities, the first Christian-Jewish communities, accepted and recognized the new church, which was born among the poor Greeks in the cities and hills. And also in our days, our faith may be renewed in contact with the new faith, the new hope, the new solidarity in the kingdom of God. The unique witness of Jesus Christ, the unique witness facing the world, the force, the strength of his spirit is so strong that in Latin America, as in other countries and continents, the testimony of the witnesses appears and is manifested in the ultimate sign of the good witness, the martyr.

Students from my own college died martyrs because they announced the true God, confronting the false god. The true God is always a God of justice, justice for the poor. Being witnesses, giving testimony to Jesus Christ, denouncing false gods, that is the task. Not only denouncing, but also announcing that God is here in this country, in this community.

In Christian communities among the poor there are thousands announcing the kingdom of Jesus Christ. To be witnesses of Jesus Christ we do not have to be rivals of the big ideologies in our world. There is no competition; Jesus Christ never, never intended to enter into a competition with the ideologies of his time. He has other signs, other manifestations and other power—the power of creating the kingdom in those persons rejected by others. That kingdom is stronger than the others, more powerful than the others, and we are witnesses to the power of God, the real power of the Spirit in our world today.

If you consider our Christianity as a system of ideas, a competition of ideas is possible. We can discuss and discuss until the end of this world and we will never arrive at a conclusion. It is not a problem of ideas or ideology. It is a problem of our reality, a real presence, a real action of Jesus Christ in this world and that is the testimony. I think the Latin American church is trying to give here and all over the world this new message. New and old, it will be the same message as always, renewed, because the action of God is always new.

11

CHRISTIAN WITNESS IN TODAY'S WORLD

Cahal B. Daly

One of the greatest statements of all time on the church as missionary is Pope Paul's Apostolic Exhortation, *Evangelii Nuntiandi, On Evangelization in the Modern World*. It is only one of the reasons whereby the late pope may, without rhetorical fancy, be called a missionary in the tradition of St. Paul himself.

This document places great stress on Christian witness. Pope Paul says:

> For the church, the first means of evangelization is the witness of an authentically Christian life, given over to God in a communion that nothing should destroy, and at the same time given to one's neighbor with limitless zeal. As we said recently to a group of lay people, modern man listens more willingly to witnesses than to teachers, and if he does listen to teachers, it is because they are witnesses. . . . It is primarily by her conduct and by her life that the church will evangelize the world, in other words, by her living witness of fidelity to the Lord Jesus—the witness of poverty and detachment, of freedom in the face of the powers of this world, in short, the witness of sanctity [Par. 41].

The pope also spoke in this document of the wordless witness of life, whereby Christians stir up irresistible questions in the hearts of those who see how they live. Christians, by the way they live and behave, in every area of their existence and relationships, should be challenging people into asking Why? Why do these Christians live like this? What is it in their faith and hope that inspires and motivates them to live like this? (see Par. 21).

In the world as it is today, the priority of witness over mere words, or at least the need for words to be backed up by witness, is more evident than ever before. Advertising and sales-talk, propaganda, whether political, ideological, or otherwise, are pervasive presences in modern Western mass culture.

Cahal B. Daly is bishop of Ardagh and Clonmacnoise.

All day long, week in, week out, we hear an endless succession of earnest, urgent, and often passionate speakers on the sound-waves and the television screens of much of the world, all of them purveying their products or their programs with a fervour and intensity which would seem more appropriate to the proclamation of the Good News of salvation. Modern men and women, and particularly young men and women, are being constantly bombarded with words and images, reinforced by all the arts of eloquence, persuasiveness, and real or simulated passionate conviction. For much of the time, modern listeners and viewers are being bribed by specious promises; for most of the time they are being flattered in their self-image and cajoled by their self-love. They are often at least half-aware that they are being manipulated for reasons which have little or nothing to do with the sincerity of the speaker or with genuine concern for the listener's or viewer's true welfare. At a time when the techniques and the tricks of salesmanship are increasingly invading the field of politics, and sometimes even affecting some forms of religious revivalism, people today develop an a priori scepticism, if not cynicism, about the promoters of any secular gospel; this often causes them to approach the preacher of the Christian gospel with the same initial scepticism. People of today, and especially the youth of today, have been so often misled by false secular messiahs that the credibility of the Christian preacher is no longer taken for granted; it has to be established. The indispensable way of establishing that credibility is by the witness of a life conformed to the truths and values of the gospel of Christ which we preach. Pope Paul puts his finger accurately on this imperative of witness. He says:

> It is often said nowadays that the present century thirsts for authenticity. Especially in regard to young people, it is said that they have a horror of the artificial or false and that they are searching above all for truth and honesty.
>
> These "signs of the times" should find us vigilant. Either tacitly or avowedly—but always forcefully—we are being asked: Do you really believe what you are proclaiming? Do you live what you believe? Do you really preach what you live? The witness of life has become more than ever an essential condition for real effectiveness in preaching. Precisely because of this we are, to a certain extent, responsible for the progress of the Gospel that we proclaim. . . .
>
> The world calls for and expects from us simplicity of life, the spirit of prayer, charity towards all, especially towards the lowly and the poor, obedience and humility, detachment and self-sacrifice. Without this mark of holiness, our word will have difficulty in touching the heart of modern man. It risks being vain and sterile [*Evangelli Nuntiandi*, Par. 76].

Early in the 1950s in a review of the writings of the French priests Godin and Michonneau, I made the criticism that these writers were veering toward a kind of anti-intellectualism in religion, underplaying the importance of intellectual presentation and defense of the faith and over-emphasizing the element of personal witness. I felt then that such writers were exaggerating the phenomenon of scepticism and suspicion as a feature of modern reaction to the spoken word. I now feel that I was mistaken. The phenomenon which was then discernible to keen observers in France has now come to characterize many in our own culture. We are living in what the French call the culture of suspicion. A speaker's sincerity is almost always presumed suspect. There is almost a suspension of belief at the outset in a speaker's truthfulness, until that truthfulness is demonstrated. The demonstration has, in great part, to do with the witness of a life lived in sincere and honest conformity with the spoken message.

Following the Vatican Council, Pope Paul emphasized the role of Christian witness to be exercised by lay people in the sphere of their secular tasks.

Pope Paul said:

The primary and immediate task [of lay people] . . . is to put to use every Christian and evangelical possibility latent but already present and active in the vast and complicated world of politics, society and economics, but also the world of culture, of the sciences and the arts, of international life, of the mass media. It also includes other realities which are open to evangelization, such as human life, the family, the education of children and adolescents, professional work, suffering. The more Gospel-inspired lay people there are engaged in these realities, clearly involved in them, competent to promote them, and conscious that they must exercise to the full their Christian powers which are often buried and suffocated, the more these realities will be at the service of the Kingdom of God and therefore of salvation in Jesus Christ [Par. 70].

The non-violent struggle for justice and for liberation of the oppressed is an important part of this Christian witness in today's world. Pope Paul spoke with piercing clarity, as Pope John Paul speaks today with equal force, of the links between Christian evangelization and liberation. Pope Paul in *Evangelii Nuntiandi* echoed the voice of the bishops, especially the bishops from the Third World, after the 1974 Synod. He spoke of

peoples engaged with all their energy in the effort and struggle to overcome everything which condemns them to remain on the margin of life, famine, chronic disease, illiteracy, poverty, injustices in international relations and especially in commercial exchanges, situations of economic and cultural neo-colonialism sometimes as cruel as the old political colonialism. The church, as the bishops repeated, has the duty to proclaim the liberation of millions of human beings, many of whom are her own children—the duty of assisting the birth of this liberation, of giving witness to it, of ensuring that it is complete. This is not foreign to evangelization.

There are unfortunately still some Christians who claim that questions of liberation and justice have to do with politics and not with religion. They feel that the concern of the church today with questions of justice is a distortion of the Christian gospel. Not a few will have been in sympathy with the thinking of the Dean of Peterhouse, Dr. E.R. Norman, who feels that, for example, the World Council of Churches' campaigns against racism and concern for liberation reflect a mistaken theology, constitute a betrayal of true Christianity, and manifest a pathetic opportunism and expediency on the part of a church which is desperately trying to conform to the fashionable ethos of the surrounding secular culture. Dr. Norman is wrong. It is precisely his own exclusively other-worldly interpretation of the message of Christ which is mistaken. The Lord's description of the Last Judgment in St. Matthew's Gospel is by itself enough to show that it is in this world of living men and women that we show the authenticity of our faith in God and of our protestations of love and service to him. Pope Paul insisted that the struggle for justice and for liberation are by no means a matter of opportunism or expediency, but are essential and immediate implications of the Gospel itself. He said:

> Between evangelization and human advancement—development and liberation—there are in fact profound links. They include links of the eminently evangelical order, which is that of charity: how in fact can one proclaim the new commandment without promoting in justice and in peace the true, authentic advancement of man? We ourselves have taken care to point this out, by recalling that it is impossible to accept that in evangelization one could or should ignore the importance of the problems so much discussed today, concerning justice, liberation, development and peace in the world. This would be to forget the lesson which comes to us from the Gospel concerning love of our neighbor who is suffering and in need [Par. 31].

With the masterly equilibrium which characterized all his teaching, Pope Paul went on to warn that "generous Christians . . . in their wish to commit the church to the liberation effort are frequently tempted to reduce her mission to the dimensions of a simply temporal project." He consequently stresses the uniqueness of the truly Christian understanding of liberation, where the primacy belongs to freedom of the spirit to seek communion with God, freedom in Christ from the oppression and unfreedom of sin. Liberation in the Christian sense cannot be separated from conversion to God in Christ. Pope Paul says:

> The church considers it to be undoubtedly important to build up structures which are more human, more just, more respectful of the rights of

the person and less oppressive and less enslaving, but she is conscious that the best structures and the most idealized systems soon become inhuman if the inhuman inclinations of the human heart are not made wholesome, if those who live in these structures or who rule them do not undergo a conversion of heart and of outlook [Par. 36].

One field which in all countries at this time urgently needs a leavening of Christian witness from lay followers of Christ is the field of politics. One of the greatest needs in today's world is for young men and women of Christian conviction and concern, of social passion and of technical competence, to involve themselves in political life. In modern society, Christian love can be made fully effective only through political action. Politics in a Christian society can be and must be charity in action, love matched by power at the service of the least of Christ's brothers and sisters.

It is in this sense that Karl Barth remarked, in his paradoxical style, that all genuine Christian preaching is also in its effect political.

"Any article of belief, any statement of doctrine, which would leave our relationship with other men and with society unaffected, would not be an article of Christian faith or a statement of Christian doctrine." Our faith is a faith that works through love. It is a truth that came into the world, not with Marx but with Christ himself, that the point of a true philosophy is not to explain the world but to change it. Chesterton may have muddled his metaphors but he did not muddle his Christian thinking when he said: "Christianity even when watered down is hot enough to boil all modern society to rags. The mere minimum of the church would be a deadly ultimatum to the world."

12

THE ROLE OF WOMEN IN THE CHURCH

Mary Motte

To approach a reflection about woman and her role in the church today calls for a stance that is sensitive to the situations emerging in the various societies of the world. A spate of literature is available on the subject of woman's emancipation in traditional types of society as well as in those areas of greater affluence and development where the tone and content are more sophisticated. We must realize, however, that no sector is far distant from another because, even though vast differences do exist, mass communication, with its elements of rapidity, intensity, and exposure, continually lessens the distance between cultural or other patterns presently existing in different societies. What is in one place today will be in another tomorrow, mingled with differing and complicating factors for better or worse.

There are several perspectives from which we can consider the history of the world. If we look at it from the biblical perspective we can see history as a series of developmental stages through which God continually calls us, this people, to new realizations. We have come to associate these signs with events, happenings, in the world around us. The mass media at our disposal make many of these events present to us in one way or another, so in a certain sense, as our knowledge and awareness increase, so does our responsibility. Once we are aware, the central focus is not events in themselves but rather *how* we respond to what is happening. In this world in which we have been called by God to live, our sins of omission cannot easily be attributed to ignorance. At times our only response can be concern, but the fact that we have allowed ourselves to become concerned makes a difference in our way of thinking and acting.

We are increasingly aware that there was and still is something marginal about women in today's world. One of the factors contributing to marginalization is the different rate of development in various sectors of society. An

Sr. Mary Motte, F.M.M., Ph.D., is an American and a member of the SEDOS Executive Committee, Rome.

ongoing evaluation process is underway, which identifies elements of marginalization among women. The process is going on in the world at large; the church's insertion into that process has been aided greatly by the Synod of Bishops in 1971 and its document, "Justice in the World." This process indicates injustices and marginalization; it also calls us beyond mere identification to action and further reflection.

At the heart of this process is the God of history, calling us in this latter part of the twentieth century to discern our role as men and women sharing responsibility for the task of evangelization in the service of the universal church. Here I will indicate some of the events which tell of women's marginalization, the responses being made by women and men, and some signs of future direction, especially in regard to our participative responsibility in the church. For having been called to share in Christ's kingly mission, each of us, "women and men of different conditions and professions, from those who occupy the highest posts in society to those who perform the simplest tasks," has the duty to require of self "exactly what we have been called to, what we have personally obliged ourselves to by God's grace, in order to respond to our vocation. This fidelity to the vocation received from God through Christ involved the joint responsibility for the church for which the Second Vatican Council wishes to educate all Christians."

EVENTS INDICATIVE OF WOMAN'S MARGINALIZATION

I have seen protest marches with women angry and excited, waving banners that proclaimed the time had come to end injustices, to change legislation governing divorce and abortion. I have heard women denounce sexism with quiet learning and deep conviction, sexism in all its varied manifestations, many of them unconscious. And I have heard and shared the anguish of women as they face the many questions which arise with regard to understanding and exercising ministries in the church, and here I am not simply referring to the question of priestly ordination.

The happenings which feed the source of these different manifestations of awareness and concern are varied. For example, after the Israeli War in 1967, the Jewish state changed the orientation of its economic development. This led to an increased demand for Arab woman labor from among the Palestinians living in Israel. Without entering into the political/justice/economic ramifications of this question, I simple wish to indicate that, regardless of cause, this situation is creating a new ambience for the Palestinian rural woman, freeing her from a centuries-old traditional role in her family, with both positive and negative results attached to that freeing. Between 1967 and 1972, seven thousand Palestinian women entered the industrial work force as development in textile and food processing industries required increased unskilled labor—precisely the labor these women were practiced in. In the dynamic process, which is not immune to questions of justice, but which occurred as these women became part of the work force, a new awareness has been coming to life among them. Who is shaping this awareness? Each situation has its own characteristics, but the process by which rural women in particular are being introduced to the economic develpment of the world is being repeated with various nuances wherever rural and underdeveloped situations exist.

The plan of action drawn up during International Women's Year indicated the need for special training programs for girls and women in rural areas, so that they would be enabled to participate fully in the economic and social growth process. Educational programs such as these have important implications, for they enable women to benefit from technical advances, and thus reduce the time formerly given to household tasks; they tend to help the woman remain in the rural area, which in turn helps to slow down the exodus to urban areas and its frequently negative, destructive implications. Studies have shown that in educating the mother, the child is helped, for it is the mother rather than the father who has a profound influence on a child's performance in school.

The increasing concern about population growth in the world has led to a persistent development of family planning programs of all kinds, and these have been effective to some extent in slowing down the population growth rate. A concrete result of these programs, particularly among poorer women, is that having smaller families they have less work and more time to themselves. How will they use this time and what effects will this change in their lifestyle have on them and on their families?

At a recent meeting of the Asian Theological Conference of the Third World Theologians in Sri Lanka (January 1979), some of the women present drew up a statement expressing their views about women's marginalization. The following quotation is taken from a draft statement, though it should be noted that not all of the women participants of the meeting agreed to this statement. My purpose in citing it is to show what some women are saying and what some see and express openly as burning issues.

We women here at the Conference and those we represent demand a recognition of and a conscious struggle against our exploitation as women and female workers, our rejection as professionally competent women, our ostracism as "single" women, our sexual vulnerability, exploited especially as political prisoners, our condemnation as prostitutes and unwed mothers, while our clients and unwed fathers of our children face no comment.

We strongly resist the domestification of women through religious devotions to the Blessed Virgin projected as frail with either upswept or downcast eyes, slender and ever youthful—the bourgeois concept of beauty and acceptance propagated through capitalist advertising. We disapprove of the excessive emphasis on purity and fidelty evolved in a puritanical society and a society needful of the assurance of the legitimacy of an heir in a property-inheriting society. We stand for devotion to Mary, consciously choosing to be the Mother of the One who would struggle fearlessly against oppressive powers and sin, at the side of her Son—Saviour in life and in death—a woman rejoicing in the exaltation of the lowly and the denuncuation of the pretentious. . . .

There are words here that may make many feel uncomfortable, and understandably so. Yet these words need to be heard if we are to speak to the sources of injustice, unrest, and marginalization so keenly felt. For, as Pope John Paul II reminds us in his encyclical *Redemptor Hominis,*

It is a noble thing to have a predisposition for understanding every person, analyzing every system and recognizing what is right; this does not at all mean losing certitude about one's own faith. . . . The missionary attitude always begins with a feeling of deep esteem for "what is in man," for what man has himself worked out in the depths of his spirit concerning the most profound and important problems. It is a question of respecting everything that has been brought about . . . by the Spirit, which "blows where it will." The mission is never destruction, but instead it is a taking up and fresh building, even if in practice there has not always been full correspondence with this high ideal.

RESPONSES BY WOMEN AND MEN

Various reactions are possible to all these cries coming from women in the world today. We can evaluate what is being asked, claimed, demanded, and write off some as contrary to our beliefs. Yet, upon reflection, no one of these cries, even that which may be most contrary to our deepest convictions, even disgusting to our sense of morality, can be simply written off. Because no one of these questions is limited to a single segment of our global society; they all, with greater or lesser intensity, penetrate to all the cultural and geographic, national and ideological layers of the world. And so none of these questions is a passing thing. They have been before us for some time. And for these reasons we are called to go beyond what we hear and see; the cries of women themselves call us to look at the driving force resulting in this rather overwhelming awareness of marginalization. We have the responsibility to make these events significant because of our commitment to the gospel.

Paul VI told us in *Evangelii Nuntiandi* that evangelizing for the church means "bringing the Good News into all the strata of humanity, and through its influence transforming humanity from within and making it new." And this because, for the church, "it is a question not only of preaching the Gospel in ever wider geographic areas or to ever greater numbers of people, but also of affecting, as it were, upsetting, through the power of the Gospel, mankind's criteria of judgment, determining values, points of interest, lines of thought, sources of inspiration and models of life, which are in contrast with the Word of God and the plan of salvation." We have always to begin with the person and "we are called to always return to relationships of people among themselves and with God."

John Paul II recalls to us that "the Church lives . . . by this truth about the human person, namely the affirmation of the body given life by the Spirit, which enables one to go beyond the bounds of temporariness and at the same time to think with particular love and solicitude of everything within the dimensions of this temporariness that affects the life of the human spirit."

Seeing ourselves at the point in which we are inserted in the human community, seeing ourselves as Christians, responsible for bringing about with others the fullness of the Kingdom, we must ask ourselves first of all, and enable others to ask, how personally and culturally the changes we have experienced in our lifestyle have engendered new kinds of relationships with men and women, have engendered conflict, how these changes have created new kinds of awareness, have brought about new kinds of work and how these in turn have affected relationships. The minutes of the Commission on Faith and Order of the World Council of Churches meeting held in Accra in 1974 contain the following recognition:

> Our Christian faith leads us to hope for a renewed and transformed man-woman relationship. In the creation God made us male and female persons, called to discover who we are and to find fullness of life through the community of men and women. Through the covenant with his people and the appeals of the prophets, God has sought to bring justice, love and peace to that community. But we recognize that sin has distorted and thwarted the full development of our man-woman relationship.

In the time which has elapsed since Vatican II, there are many events that have become significant for us in different sectors of church life because of the responses being made. I will limit my examples to the area of evangelization and cite a few of these events in a general way, events which have had in many instances multiple effects. From the response being made, it should be possible to indicate directions for the future.

There has been a continuous effort to include women in the various activities related to church life, from which they were either always or usually excluded in the past. At times this inclusion can smack of tokenism: "We have to have a woman to avoid being criticized." Sometimes the efforts have been made only because of pressure and prodding. But in the midst of it all, two factors are emerging: (1) women are contributing to the life of the church in new ways as compared with the past; (2) their contributions are proving adequate and tending to encourage genuine efforts to extend other invitations and appointments to women. There is still more to be done.

Another surge forward in the task of evangelization has come about because of the reflection thrust upon all of us by Vatican II—painful though that reflection has been at times. With its request for renewal, which forced us to examine our lives in the light of the gospel, Vatican II laid before us the realization that new forms of insertion were being called for by the changes that had come about in society, if the presence and proclamation of the Good News were to penetrate effectively the new world that had come into being since the Second World War. It is easy to speak of this experience now, but to say we own this experience, presupposes that we know in the depths of our hearts what it has cost us to let go of what we had known, to let go of what we seemed to have been called to, to risk the unknown. We know how we had to grope, at times with little support, and we still have some poignant memories. But accompanying this experience, whether at the level of episcopal conferences in some countries, or among lay or religious in others, there has been a growing awareness that large groups of persons are not hearing the Gospel message in a way they can understand in their lives.

For many reasons women and men, more aware of their shared responsibility in the task of evangelization, have begun to move into areas of society in ways that have little or no precedent. Some failures have been noted; some successes too. But now, with a certain time of experience behind us, we can see what is emerging. Teams of men and women, priests, religious, and lay, are discovering together their own ongoing need for conversion, and the call coming from the heart of that continual conversion, to share their faith with others, to find new ways of reaching out to the non-evangelized, and to those who need support in the faith received at baptism, but never reinforced or enabled to grow. In some places these teams function as mobile units, moving around as needed; others are at the heart of basic Christian communities, and still others are small communities of Christian presence in lands of other religions.

In other instances the trend has been strongly characterized by a growth in small group living, particularly among priests or religious of a community. This style of life facilitates a going out to others; it helps to develop a new type of relationship with others, one characterized by openness to the giftedness of persons, the presence of God's spirit at work in each one, and a growing sensitivity to receiving before giving.

ORIENTATIONS FOR THE FUTURE

Seeing history from the biblical perspective enables us to experience the continual call of God and leads us to new realizations in his creation. In bringing his people out of Egypt, in giving them a personality and in freeing them, God's action has been described as a great act of motherly love. On the other hand, his action is described as fatherly love when he gives his people government and insists upon the promotion of justice through law. When we consider the experiences, some of which I have indicated in a very general way, that are emerging in the life and ministry of the church, and therefore in our own lives, we see that men and women are involved and committed together. And today I believe there is a developing sensitivity evident with regard to the values contributed by each to the work of evangelization. The task still lies before us to identify these values and thus free them from cultural or other overtones, which have accumulated with time, and which have obscured these values of being male and female, or which have falsified them due to erroneous understandings. Among many things helping in the identification and differentiation process is the increasing number of women participating in direct pastoral ministry and in new ministries. An obstacle to the process is a negative response on our part when we refuse to recognize marginalization in our lives, when we refuse to go beyond marginalization, to discover the place where, as women and men, each with unique gifts, in profound mutual respect, we give ourselves to the service of evangelization for the building up of the Kingdom.

As our experience grows in sharing in the life and ministry of the church, bringing the message of the gospel to other men and women, we come to understand better the gifts we share, the values we need to share, if the Word of God is to be heard and acted upon in today's world. Ministry and evangelization is proving to be one of the main areas in the church, which, in removing marginalized attitudes and actions from women's contribution (as well as from that of the laity in general), is opening to all of us a wider comprehension of the human person that includes a diversity of masculine and feminine characteristics in the context of a deepened spirituality shaped by experience. This spirituality is a growing awareness of God's action in history, of his presence to us now, and, in him, of our presence to one another, women and men in the church, called to hear God speaking to us now to assist him in this task of a new creation, to bring about the fullness of the Kingdom in the lives of our sisters and brothers.

CONCLUSION

My earliest prayer to Mary is associated with a small white stone statue of Our Lady of Grace, which my mother told me came from Ireland and which I understood she valued very much. When I saw this statue again recently I realized it was very simple. But to my child's mind, unconsciously absorbing devotion to Mary which my mother shared with me, it was a rather extraordinary statue. Each of us, woman or man, can go back to the beginning of our awareness of Mary and trace rather rapidly the way we have come to understand, love, and be inspired by her.

The Gospels tell us little, but enough to allow us to see her in a series of relationships with other persons: with God, letting him have his way in spite of her fears, her unanswered questions; willing to trust and risk in a situation fraught with risk and demanding a trust from the depths of a profound faith. Mary sharing her joy with Elizabeth, and so given up to the power of God, the Spirit could stir the unborn John and fill his mother, Elizabeth. Mary with Joseph, looking for the child Jesus. Mary with her son at Cana, caring about others and helping him to be concerned. Mary at Calvary believing in this child of hers when no external sign could reinforce her faith and trust; perhaps only a mother or father can begin to understand that love and fidelity born in deepest sorrow.

Maybe what the Gospels have not told of Mary would be the ordinary details of everyday life for a Jewish woman in her time. What the Gospels do tell us through the inspired writers are the very points where Mary, whom God chose to begin a significant era of the history of salvation, breaks beyond what is ordinary and forecasts as it were the new ways of relating in an attitude of deep respect. These ways will form the foundation of a new community of women and men. It would seem that today we are now being called to realize a significant step in the bringing about of this community.

13

BASIC CHRISTIAN COMMUNITIES

Brian Hearne

The idea of small Christian communities is essentially a spirituality. It is not just a pastoral strategy; it is not something which we, the church leaders, are going to do for others. It is something, first of all, which we have to do for ourselves.

The theology of Christian communities is essentially about how I live with other people, with all the practical implications that that involves.

We shouldn't make Christian communities into yet another ideology. We should see them simply as the expression of the search for communion at all levels, the search for reconciliation. Maybe it is about time we began to see how all those ways can be brought together in life: the communion of saints, the church as a communion, and Holy Communion in the Eucharist. What we are talking about is spirituality.

I would like to outline the process of both thought and action which has gone on in the countries of East Africa over the last few years, and which has led to this decisive option in pastoral practice.

What pastoral plan are we aiming at? What kind of church are we actually developing or continuing? Can we identify the model that is being used and can we discern more clearly some of the problems in it? And can we see other possibilities in such a way that there could be a movement towards a decisive change in basic pastoral approaches to respond to the needs of today?

These are the questions that have been raised in AMECEA. AMECEA is the Association of Member Episcopal Conferences of East Africa. It is comprised of bishops from seven countries—Ethiopia, Sudan, Kenya, Tanzania, Uganda, Malawi, and Zambia, and it represents quite a good cross section of East Africa. The bishops of Kenya, by their contact with the bishops of Tanzania, have been forced to see that there are certain changes going on in the church of Tanzania, which challenge the church in Kenya and vice versa. The forces of interaction are a very important element in the kind of historical development I want to try to outline.

The point of departure is Vatican II; in fact it was during Vatican II that

Fr. Brian Hearne, C.S.Sp., is professor of pastoral theology at the Gaba Institute, Kenya.

AMECEA was born. The bishops attending the council from the countries of East Africa saw that there was a real need to try and pool their resources, to come together in a creative way to implement what was happening in Vatican II. There was need of a definite plan and this was the first step they took.

There were some points in particular made at Vatican II concerning the doctrine of the church that are important. The first one is the church as the people of God. *Lumen Gentium* of Vatican II centered its theology of the church on the church as the people of God. So the question arises: in practice what do you do to make this theoretical and theological assumption a lived reality?

There were significant developments in the pastoral ministry of the church following the Arian heresy and the removal of Christ from the midst of the community, the entry of huge crowds of often half-converted people into the church, and the growth of infant baptism as the norm. The church became a church of huge numbers, and of course appropriate structures had to be developed to cater to that. What happened was the development of the parish system and the clericalization of the church. The parish system is what is called in pastoral theology a come and care system. That is, the church is set up in a place; it has its officials and they provide necessary services to the people who come for those services. So you have a rather static image of the church: the parish church becomes the center, people have to come to it, and when they come there, there are services available to them. If people want to be baptized or have their children baptized, they come to the church and they get that service. If they want the sacrament of penance they come to the church and they confess their sins and they receive the sacrament of penance. If they want to receive the Holy Eucharist they come to the church. The church obliges people to come on Sundays to fulfill the commandment of worship.

So, the system is a come and care system. In many respects it is a good system, we mustn't question that. It has done enormous good to the church but there are also some serious disadvantages in it. The first problem is: what about the people who don't come? It becomes a very big pastoral problem in many areas when we lose touch with people who don't come to church on Sunday.

The second and more profound disadvantage of this system is that it tends to increase passivity on the part of the people. People in a big crowd tend to become passive, at least a large number of them. The system is one of the people receiving the whole time. "Getting things from someone who is giving things well" is the definition of passivity. The cry for active participation is an attempt to respond to the fact that the mass of Christian people during the liturgy are purely passive. In a small group it is quite possible for all of us to be active, for all of us to express ourselves. If we want to decrease passivity and increase active involvement, we have to get down to small groups. In the Synod of 1977, there was a lot of discussion on this in connection with some of the propositions the bishops voted on. These included four or five on the parish and one of them said, "the ideal way of renewing a parish is to make it a community of communities."

The sacramental system must also be mentioned here, in particular the notion of the sacramental ministry as one which is essentially concerned with priests giving things, instead of giving sufficient attention to the fact that the sacraments are encounters, that they are actually interpersonal meetings, and that they must therefore necessarily involve a whole active participation on the part of the recipient. We don't strictly speaking receive sacraments, we celebrate sacraments. We are involved in the sacrament itself. Sacraments cause by their meaning and we are part of the meaning of the sacrament. The sacrament becomes the meeting place between the grace of Christ and our own situation, where we are as individuals and as communities, and we are part of it. So, practically speaking, to develop that notion of active participation in the sacraments leads to lots of slightly different emphases.

It leads to a much more careful catechumenal process, aiming at a very active and deliberate commitment on the part of the Christian or the would-be Christian. The rite for adult baptism stipulates that the catechumens not go from one stage to the next until they have shown an adequate degree of understanding and commitment in their life, "even if it takes many years."

These then are some of the questions behind the Vatican Council's emphasis on the church as people of God. Now we can turn to another point made at Vatican II: the theology of the local church.

Karl Rahner has written that in his view the most significant thing Vatican II says about the church is precisely what it says about the local church. While it is not true to say that Vatican II spent a lot of time talking about the local church, *Lumen Gentium* does say, in no. 26, that it is from the local church that the one and only Catholic church comes into being. Not the other way round. In mission terms it might have been a question of bringing the church, the universal church, to a given situation. According to Vatican II, it is the other way round. It is precisely as the church develops in local areas that the universal church comes into being more fully.

The important point is that the local church itself is where the mystery of the universal church is concretely lived and experienced. The working paper for the Synod of 1974 says that the local Christian communities are the places where the church actually becomes present to people.

As an example take a statement like "God is everywhere." We all know that God is everywhere, but only when that statement comes from an experience in which I can say God is here, is the mystery of God here and now among us. Only then I can say that it is true everywhere. Unless I can put it like that, the statement is empty; it has no reference point. Too often in the church we tend to speak in general terms without the particular reference. In other words we lose concreteness, we lose meaning, in the proper sense of the word. We speak about the Catholic church, the universal church, the worldwide church, but unless we have an experience of what that means in a given place it can be an empty or skeletal statement. The skeleton is the institution, the flesh and blood is the life of the local church, the living cell. In this tension between the universal and the local, the ecclesial problem of small communities can find its resolution.

We have the universal church which is the Catholic church and which is presided over by the pope, the bishop of Rome. The pope is the center of unity for all local churches. The principle here is precisely the principle of communion. I think it is a useful way of looking at the ecclesial nature of the small community. It can answer some of those questions about the elitist problem, about the closed group problem, that are usually mentioned when people talk of small communities. Now since Vatican II with its emphasis on cultures, not just one culture, and the need for the Church to be incarnated in different cultures (particularly as in section 3 of *Ad Gentes*) there has been a very interesting development at the structural level. Already you can see, not a canonical structure, but a real live structure beginning to develop where the experience of church is now taking a particular shape.

The universal church is seen more clearly now as being incarnate in different regional churches. Here I mean region in the widest sense; for example, Latin America. We even have structures beginning to correspond to this— CELAM, AMECEA, and the Asian Bishops Conference.

These are developments which are new and are the result of the emphasis of Vatican II on localizing the church. So the regional church has come into being, a church with a common culture, we could say.

There are a lot of obscure areas still, but there is something developing in the church at the moment. One can envision the church of the future as a system of patriarchates—the patriarchate of Africa, the patriarchate of India, the patriarchate of Latin America, the partriarchate of the United States. One of the pope's titles is Patriarch of the West—Patriarch of the West, but not universal Patriarch. That system of patriarchates could well be the structural expression of the new emphasis on incarnating the church in different cultures, just as the ancient church was really a communion of communions in which the pope was the hinge, as it were, the visible center. To be in communion with the pope, the bishop of Rome, was to be in communion with all the other local churches. That idea could well be emerging once again in the church.

This is the kind of thing we are actually living through; it is so close to us we don't see it, but it is beginning to happen, slowly and painfully, with a certain amount of tension. There is a good bit of tension between, for example, the Office of Propaganda Fide in Rome and the above-named regional organizations. Propaganda Fide is essentially a centralized organ; the other organizations are not centralized, they are localized.

At Vatican II the local church was early on defined in terms of the diocese. The document on liturgy (no. 41) stated, "the clearest manifestation of the church of Christ on earth is the celebration of the Eucharist by the bishop in his cathedral surrounded by his priests and people." Now that is an interesting concept but it is a very unsatisfactory one for many reasons. For example,

I could ask Bishop Ndingi, how many people can actually fit into your cathedral, and how many people would have to stay outside? If the local church is defined in terms of the Eucharistic celebration, but in such a way that by definition the vast majority of the Christians in that community are excluded, the definition must be reexamined.

The concept of the diocese as the local church is both valid and valuable. It corresponds to the need of people to belong to a wider grouping which is still not too wide, where they can feel more or less at home. For example, in Nakuru diocese people know they belong to Nakuru diocese even if they live quite far from Nakuru town, quite far from the bishop. There is that sense of belonging to a wider unity, and this is important. But perhaps it isn't sufficient to just follow the definition of Vatican II. We have to go further to discover the truly local church.

The next step is to the parish. But the same problem arises there. We find that in most parishes we have to have several Eucharistic celebrations on Sundays because of the large number of people coming to them. We have to ask: is that really a community as opposed to a gathering, a society, an organization? Obviously there is a focal point of community building at this center—people are doing the same thing. But you could say the same thing of a football match. When people come to watch a football match, whether there are four thousand or two thousand doesn't matter all that much. There is a kind of unity among the crowd. So the parish is itself already too big and I think that is what the Synod meant when it said something like, "Most parishes in the church are in need of renewal because they are not able to adequately respond to the spiritual needs of the people."

That is a clear statement. We must remember too that originally in the church the bishop was the only one who presided over the Eucharist—the only one—and it was only with growing numbers that bishops had to delegate authority over the Eucharist to priests. We can say there was a breakdown from the original structure of the diocese to parishes within the diocese. We now find the parish system is also unsatisfactory in certain respects. It can be improved so we are simply going a stage further.

Now there is a problem here. In most African parishes we have outstations. But even outstations are not what is meant by a small Christian community. In some cases they may be, but they are really villages or areas that depend on the parish for the priest to come and say Mass. So basically it is still the come and care system. The problem being faced here is how to get down to a further level of the church itself. Not just to form another little group, a sodality, an action group or a prayer group, but how the mystery of the church itself can be further localized so that people don't have to come and "be cared for," so that people experience the church where they are. And I think this is the fundamental idea behind the breaking up of the parish or the outstation further, into small communities.

This has proved useful in many places for various reasons. It shows that the small communities were the most local incarnation of the universal church; it shows that they in no way replaced the parish. Here I think I am being faithful to the thinking of the AMECEA bishops. In some parts of the world it has been suggested that small communities will replace the parish. I don't think that that is what is meant in the AMECEA policy of small communities. It is more along the lines of the Synod statement of making the parish into a community of communities. While the small communities have their own life they are also reaching out to one another and have the opportunity to meet as parish from time to time, on a wider scale.

I think we have an important principle here. It is once again the principle of communion, which means linking up. It means that in all structures there has to be a vital principle of reaching out to other levels, both horizontally and vertically. For example, the regional churches have got to be in communion with one another. There has to be contact, there has to be sharing at various levels—theological, spiritual, and pastoral—between the churches of the world as they develop into more clearly distinct regional churches. This is in order that there may be interaction between them, so that there may be a mutual learning, so that for the good of all there may be growth and renewal. Vertically, you can visualize a system of arrows, pointing out in every direction.

In the diocesan church there also has to be a reaching out to the regional church and to other dioceses, some kind of principle of communion. This, of course, is based theologically on the collegiality of bishops. Ultimately the expression of the unity of the local church is in the collegiality of the bishops, who are truly representing their local churches. A lot of work has to be done with regard to parishes. As for the relationship among parishes, is there anything in the parish churches that facilitates the sharing of parish priests? The deanery is one example, but there are possibilities at all levels. In small communities there is the need to relate to the parish and for parishes to relate to one another if they are truly to be the most local expressions of the church. It is useful to put into context some of the problems that come up. For example, if you say that small communities are just for a few people, Bishop Christopher Mwoleka of Tanzania would vigorously object. He would say, "No, they are for all the believing faithful, because they are the ways the church is made real to the people. They are not optional groups." So, in a sense, if someone does not belong to the church at the most local level you can question his or her belonging to the church at all, in terms of commitment, in terms of service, in terms of ministry, in terms of responsibility.

The third point from Vatican II is the church as a place of dialogue. According to the Council the church can no longer see itself as a closed group. It has to be open to the world, to be open to other religions, it has to be open to other churches. At the end of *Gaudium et Spes*, Pope Paul's *Ecclesiam Suam* is summarized: "The church has to be in dialogue within itself." Here is what that means in practice: the church has to be in dialogue with other churches, it has to be in dialogue with other religions, and of course this is a profoundly important thing for missionary work today. It has to be in dialogue with everything that is of value in the cultures even of unbelievers. We exclude nobody from this dialogue.

We are committed to taking the initiative. In that context I have a few remarks to make. The first is that if that is the true image of the church in Vatican II, it must be the image of the church here and now because this is the church, the most local realization of the church. So the small community has to be a place of dialogue and service, it is not to be a closed group.

The second point comes back to what was said in the beginning: our spirituality. What was said of the church there has also to be said of each member of the church—otherwise it doesn't make sense. So each one of us has, as it were, to take that as our own personal character of spirituality. There is no easy way out. We have to be honest with ourselves, admit the number of people we continually refuse to be in dialogue with, and do something about it. Can I say of myself that I exclude nobody from dialogue with me? At least I should be struggling towards that if my spirituality is in tune with what Vatican II says of the church. Theology, pastoral practice, and spirituality: they are all the same when it comes to practice. To make a theological statement one must somehow come down to the gut level; if it doesn't come to that, it is irrelevant.

14

BASIC COMMUNITIES:
THE AFRICAN EXPERIENCE

Raphael Ndingi

Since I am a bishop from Kenya, I cannot speak for the whole continent of Africa. There are over forty countries in Africa—far more than there are in Europe. I can, however, speak for more than just Kenya. We are fortunate in the church in Kenya to have gone beyond our national boundaries and to have joined with six other countries to form an Association of Bishops' Conferences in Eastern Africa called AMECEA. This happened eighteen years ago and ever since then the bishops have been meeting every three years to discuss the situation in the church in our part of the world. In 1973 we tried to project what the situation would be like in 1980 and to ask ourselves what steps we should take so we would be prepared.

It was at that meeting in 1973 that we began to realize that the structure we had in the church would not be sufficient for the 1980s. It was good for administration, but it did not go down deeply enough. It had evolved over the years when there were few missionaries and large areas to cover. It included episcopal conferences, dioceses, parishes, and usually outstations, which were subdivisions of the parish and were periodically visited by the priest. These *outstations* often covered many square miles.

It is true that our Christians gathered at the outstations, especially when the priest came, to attend Mass and receive the sacraments. Many of them also gathered there on Sundays and feast days to pray together, to sing hymns, to listen to the Scripture readings for that day and, under the guidance of the catechist or local church leader, to receive further religious instruction and to take some action to improve the standard of Christian life among their members. All this was good and perhaps all we could have expected under the circumstances that prevailed up until then.

However, in 1973 we began to realize that it was not in these outstations that our people lived their Christian commitment. They came to these outstations to offer public worship to God and to receive the sacraments and

Raphael Ndingi is bishop of Nakuru, Kenya.

further instructions and this was both good and necessary, but they lived out their daily Christian commitment elsewhere. They lived it where they lived; they lived it in their own neighborhoods.

We were convinced, therefore, that *church life must be based on these neighborhoods (communities) in which everyday life and work take place:* those small and manageable social groupings whose members can experience real interpersonal relationships and feel a sense of communal belonging, both in living and working. We believed that Christian communities at this level would be best suited to develop real vitality and to become effective witnesses in their natural environment.

That was in 1973. Over the next three years the idea grew. I must add that it grew quite independently of the fact that the same idea was growing in South America and other places throughout the world, since we had had very little communication with those places. Call it what you will, but I call it the workings of the Holy Spirit in the church. By 1976 when it became time for all the bishops of East Africa to assemble again, the idea had taken on such importance that we decided to hold our study conference exclusively on this subject of building small Christian communities. We did not call them "basic" like they did in South America, but "small." I don't know exacly why we used "small" instead of "basic," but it is another indication that the movement in Africa was growing on its own, quite independent of what was happening along the same lines in other places.

Perhaps we used the word "'small" because that is exactly what we meant. We had come to realize that our people live out their Christian commitment in "small" communities where they could know one another and relate to one another. They could, of course, relate to one another when they came to the parish or outstation for Mass. They related to one another as Christians all sharing the same faith, and all offering public worship to God as a wider community, and this they still do. But they could not relate to one another in a personal way since they were so many.

To relate to one another in a personal way demanded smaller communities. These smaller communities, we felt, should be built on units that already existed in our local society, not on artificial structures imposed from the outside. During our 1976 meeting, we identified these exisiting units in our local society as groups built on clan relationships, people doing the same kind of work or engaged in the same profession, or coming from the same area and now living in our towns and cities. For the vast majority of our people, interpersonal relationships were enjoyed on a day-to-day basis by those who physically lived near one another in the same neighborhood. By "small" Christian communities we therefore meant mainly neighborhood Christian communities—people who knew one another, lived close to one another and could relate to one another day to day as they lived out their Christian commitment.

At this level, the needs and problems of the church are of smaller dimension, and the involvement of the community in working toward solutions is most readily achieved.

In 1974 a Synod was held in Rome on evangelization. When the bishops from East Africa went to Rome and began speaking about small Christian communities, some bishops from other parts of the world did not know what they were talking about. They thought our bishops were talking about fringe groups—groups of Christians on the fringe of church structure—or underground communities that were doing their own thing their own way. It was only later that those other bishops came to realize more exactly what we meant by small Christian communities in Africa, and then they became interested. Our bishops also became interested when they realized that similar developments were taking place in the church in other parts of the world. Small communities became so much a part of the Synod that Pope Paul VI devoted an entire section to them in *Evangelii Nuntiandi*.

Our concept in East Africa of small Christian communities was so far removed from the fringe mentality that we began to see these communities as the groundwork for the structure of the whole church.

In the past, it was common to picture the church as a triangle with the pope on top, followed by the bishops, the clergy, the religious, and the laity on the bottom; an arrow pointed downwards implying that everything came from the top down.

I am aware that authority comes from above, but then authority that provides leadership, direction, and coordination takes into account the family (community) that it has charge of. Such authority establishes a kind of Holy Spirit. Yet they are Three in One, and One in Three.

In East Africa a new approach to ecclesiology is evolving. It is based on the concept of the church as a communion of communities, a two-way sharing between communities, while at the same time preserving everyone's Christ-given role within the church, including the roles of the pope and bishops.

Instead of starting the groundwork with the parish, as we did formerly, we start it with the small communities. The parish, after all, is not where the pastor happens to live but a whole area. This whole area is subdivided into neighborhoods and each of these neighborhoods forms a small Christian community. The parish then becomes a communion of these small Christian communities with the pastor as the shepherd of all the communities. The communion of communities on the parish level enjoys a two-way sharing. The small communities, through their representatives, feed their thinking, problems and experiences up to the parish level, either directly, or, in cases of a parish with a large area, through outstation councils, which are represented on the parish council. The pastor and the parish council, in turn, receive such thinking, problems, and experiences from all the small communities in the area, review them and are enriched by them. After decisions are taken at the parish level, they can then be shared with all the small communities through the representatives at the parish council. Through this same means, good experiences of one particular community can be also shared with all the other communities in the parish; and the parish becomes a living communion of communities.

In the same way, all the parishes in the diocese become a communion of communities on the diocesan level with the bishop as the shepherd of all the communities. The dioceses in turn become a communion of communities forming the episcopal (or bishops') conference for the entire nation. In this way there is a living chain from the neighborhood Christian community right up to the bishops' conference and from the bishops' conference to the neighborhood community.

The national bishops' conferences in our church do not exist in isolation. They form part of the universal church and are linked to each other through union with the Holy Father who is the supreme shepherd for the whole church. In this way, the whole church is a living communion of communities. At least, this is the way we see it in East Africa.

Now let's go back to the neighborhood community, the small Christian community. Just exactly what is it, how is it formed, and how does it operate?

Recently the diocese of Zambia described what they meant by a small Christian community. Their combined definition reads: "A small or basic Christian communitiy is a group of convinced and committed Christians who feel related, who together deepen and live their commitment to Jesus Christ and the Christian way of life."

The combined report went on to say:

> Membership is small enough for people to know each other and feel a sense of belonging. At the same time numerous enough to find among themselves the leaders needed to carry out their mission both within and outside their community. The communities in turn become evangelizing agents to the people around them.
>
> The small community brings people of a small neighborhood together and they begin to experience for the first time the meaning of Christian brotherhood, by helping people to meet on an inter-personal level and by beginning to translate the Christian message into practical actions to meet each other's needs.

All this, of course, fits in very well with our traditional African background where "family and extended family relationships are of great value . . . a sense of belonging, a strong unity and mutual service and protection." The Zambia report goes on to state:

> Apart from a few active members in the parish, the majority of the parishioners are, by and large, passive receivers of the ministrations of the priest and take no responsibility for the policy and direction of the church or for the evangelization of the people around them. Their Christian faith has little influence on the life they live everyday.

This is the way it was in most parishes throughout East Africa, and this is the way it is yet today in some of them. In others, however, the situation is changing. The initial change came through the establishment of parish councils, but the bigger change is coming through the establishment of small Christian communities. The number of these small Christian communities differs from diocese to diocese. Some dioceses have as many as eight hundred groups, while others have only two hundred. Gradually they are spreading through East Africa; building them has become the pastoral priority of the AMECEA bishops.

But how does one go about forming these small Christian communities? So far, we see two different ways: either animating the Christians of our parishes to group themselves into small communities from which leaders surface, or starting with training known leaders who in turn gather small communities around them. There may be other ways, but they have not yet evolved in our part of the world.

What often happens is that Christians in a neighborhood start gathering together at someone's house to pray together. I'm told this has also happened through the charismatic movement, but the charismatic members are not necessarily from the same neighborhood. Another difference between the small Christian communities and the charismatic movement seems to be that the latter is a particular approach to prayer and sharing that appeals only to certain people; whereas the small Christian communities are meant to be the groundwork of church structure and are therefore the basic cell for all the Christians in the neighborhood. No doubt there are other differences, but let me say here that small Christian communities are not in competition with other movements and societies in the church which are usually on the parish level and not on a neighborhood level. Such movements and societies will continue to meet regularly at the parish level where they will become a link between the different Christian communities and help prevent them from adopting a "ghetto" spirit. Some of the leaders of these parish societies have also become leaders in the evolving Christian communities.

I say the Christian communities are evolving. As they evolve under the guidance of the Spirit, we are coming to a clearer notion of just what they are to be. There is no predetermined plan on what they should be and it is possible they will differ somewhat from one area to another.

Usually after the Christians in a neighborhood start gathering together to pray together, they start reading Scripture together and sharing their thoughts on the passage read. In all the cases I know of, this Scripture sharing always takes a practical turn; these people apply the Scripture passage to their own life situation. It has happened, however, in at least one place, that Scripture sharing was over-emphasized to the detriment of other goals of small Christian communities.

As with prayer and Scripture sharing, these other goals arise from the fact that the motivation behind forming a small Christian community is the fact that it is a faith community. It is faith, not structure, that motivates. As a faith community that is Christ-centered, the faith of its members should be renewed, sustained, nourished, and helped to grow so that it will give deeper meaning and direction to their lives.

In such a community, the members share their joys, sorrows, and problems of daily life with one another and together try to solve these problems in the light of the common faith of their members.

One of these problems can be the need for reconciliation between the members of the community itself or between others. If the members are open, approachable, simple, and people of faith, they should be able to go far in the ministry of reconciliation. In certain parts of the world, this is ministry that is very needed today.

Another ministry that is very much needed is that of religious education. In many countries, both in Africa and other lands, the youth are not receiving sufficient religious formation, and sometimes none at all, in the schools. Much of this can be supplemented by someone selected within the small Christian community to give this religious formation. The formation should not be limited to youth. The very notion of a small Christian community is a group of Christians that deepens the Christian life of all its members, including the adults.

The nature of the community also calls for other lay ministries. Since it is a community that prays together, it needs a prayer leader. It needs an animator and someone to foster the sacramental life of its members, especially the way they are living the sacrament of matrimony. It needs an extraordinary minister of the Eucharist, and it may on occasion invite the priest to offer Mass within the community. Other lay ministries may evolve as the need arises.

All these lay ministries normally would not be perfomed by the same person, since they depend on the particular charism given to different individuals. We are finding in East Africa that this is a great improvement over the old system when everything was done by the priest or in the outstation by the catechist. We depended too much on the catechists. They were normally dependable, but if they went, everything went with them. The catechist is still needed, and very much needed, but we must also involve other members of the community and their God-given charisms in the apostolate.

As lay ministries continue to evolve, we should be careful not to call everything a layperson does a "lay ministry"; otherwise the term would soon become so vague that it would lose its meaning. In East Africa we distinguish between ministries and services. Many things, such as financial and material matters, fall under services.

Although it is hoped people with potential charisma will be found in all small communities for these ministries and services, they need to be developed and formed. They should not be chosen too quickly. There should be firm grounds that they themselves are living good Christian lives, and have at least the potential qualities for the functions they are to perform. Then they need training. Leaders, in particular, need this training so that they will be able to draw out potential qualities in other members of the community and be able to make good decisions, execute them, and then evaluate the results.

There should also be training for those performing the other ministries and services in the community. But how can all this training be given, especially if there are hundreds of such communities in a given area?

This depends to a great extent on what method the bishop of the diocese decides to adopt. There are many options: leadership training centers, seminars, retreats, workshops, the use of printed manuals, teams that go through the diocese offering training. In one area of Africa, leaders were trained and they in turn trained others. In Rulenge diocese in Tanzania, a year was set aside to train each category of ministries and services throughout the whole diocese. In 1976 they had seminars in the diocese on establishing small Christian communities. In 1977 they trained prayer leaders. Last year they trained religious formation leaders. This year they are training those in charge of financial matters, especially in view of self-reliance. Next year there will be another group.

These ministries and services are geared towards the small Christian community which, while remaining small enough for interpersonal relations, should be large enough to provide the ministries and services it needs within itself. I would say, however, that each individual community does not have to supply each and every possible lay ministry and service it might need. Some of these could be supplied by a group of communities getting together and selecting people to offer their services to the communities within that group; for instance, a well-trained catechist, an extraordinary minister of the Eucharist.

All involved should remember that they have formed themselves into a small Christian community not just for the members of that community but also for the good of the wider community. As it has already been pointed out, we must not let a "ghetto" mentality develop. Each community must reach out to the wider community: the Christians in neighboring communities, the outstation, the parish, the diocese, the universal church. They should also reach out to the general society in which they live, and see what they can do to better it.

No small Christian community should live in isolation, no matter how far away it may be from other Christians. If it does, the situation harbors great dangers. The community removes itself from the mainstream of the church, its thinking and its way of life. It can easily become a fringe group and may even go completely astray. In Africa, there is real danger that it could end up becoming another independent church. This has happened in the past in Kenya when Praesidia of the Legion of Mary in one section became cut off from the mainstream of the church and formed themselves into the independent church known as the Maria Legio.

This danger must be avoided at all costs. No matter how many small Christian communities are established in a parish, each one of them must be kept within the mainstream of the church. One way of doing this is to have a mobile team of priests, sisters, catechists, and other trained persons constantly visiting the various communities in a parish as individuals or as a team, to see how they are developing and to give them deeper insights. Another way is to circulate printed literature to them from the parish or diocesan offices to further their instructions. But above all, the two-way communication I mentioned in connection with the evolving view on ecclesiology must be maintained. Each and every small Christian community must have its representation in a higher body, be it an outstation council or the parish council. If there are too many communities for each to have its own representative, then one person from the area could represent several communities, but he or she must know what is happening in each of those communities and report back to each of them after the council meeting. Church leaders, be they bishops, parish priests, parish council members, or other lay leaders, should see to it that this is done in an ongoing manner.

There are dangers in establishing small Christian communities, but there are also ways of overcoming them. Such dangers should not lessen our pastoral initiative to establish and deepen these small Christian communities. Christ has told us that where two or three are gathered in his name, he is in their midst. They are part of his Mystical Body, the church. All does not depend on us. We should leave something to the Holy Spirit who dwells in the church and therefore, in its members in these small communities. He gives them life. He gives them light. He gives them guidance. He gives them love, so that in their own neighborhoods they can raise the sign of God's presence.

15

A LAYMAN'S VIEW
OF THE FUTURE OF MISSION

August Vanistaendal

One day a study should be done on the relationship between pessimism and puritanism. A rather distinguished American professor once gave me the following definition of a puritan: a person who is afraid that somewhere, sometime, somehow, somebody might be happy! We know that we are sinners, that we have to grope for truth, but we also know that we are the bearers of a message of compassion, of love, of liberation for all people of all races, however humble and poor they may seem to be. Certainly we should not indulge in naive triumphalism; but don't we have an indestructible hope, an eternal, inalienable promise, an unshakeable certainty which is called faith?

It is wonderful to behold the real living church and to sense that mission is not an exotic exercise but a living reality, a permanent challenge for each one of us, for every Christian in Ireland, in my own dear Flanders, in Europe, in Africa, Asia, Australia, and the Americas.

Three small countries have, in the past, been the home countries of more than half of all the missionaries sent out to preach the Gospel—Ireland, Holland, and my own Belgium. Of these Ireland undoubtedly has the most ancient missionary tradition, since Irish missionaries went to both Holland and Belgium to spread Christianity in early times. One might conclude that it was the original Irish touch which made the two other countries so fertile in missionary vocations. Thousands of our brothers and sisters answered the call of the Lord and went overseas to preach the gospel. They were the missionaries of the heroic times, which came to an end rather abruptly with the independence of former colonial territories. However, even if regimes change, the mission entrusted to us by Christ goes on.

Not only the pace of history but also the pace of technology has quickened. We are the people of the jet age. We have no time for romantic decorum. We no longer have Latin as a symbol of unity. To us religion is no longer comparable to a social security system for eternity under the administration of the

August Vanistaendal is chairman of Pro Mundi Vita, Brussels, of Caritas, Belgium, and former director of the Catholic Trade Unions of Belgium.

Almighty. We experience that it is more difficult for the rich to understand and follow the Gospel message than it is for the poor. Some have announced that God is dead; others proclaim that our generation is no longer in need of the supernatural. And yet how could this be? The present we live in and the future before us offer us the real, practical possibility of going to the end of the world, of reaching out to all human beings of all nations, cultures, languages, races, and colors, because, for the very first time in the history of mankind, technology allows us to do so. Jets cross the air from north to south, from east to west, leaving no place undetected or undisturbed. This indeed, far from being the end of mission, should be the golden age of mission. For the first time in human history the psalm will come true: "Laudate Dominum omnes gentes, laudate eum omnes populi." Because his compassion for us has been proven. For the first time in history the boundaries of charity and justice extend to the ends of the earth. And for the first time the home communities of missionaries will almost simultaneously be informed about what is happening.

However, this will require a different approach from that of the past. In the past the whole Christian community took it for granted that missionaries were carrying out their missionary obligation for them and felt happy to be rid of it. In the future, mission will become again a matter for the whole Christian community, as it always should have been. At present we witness a rather timid beginning of lay participation in missionary activities on a volunteer basis. Responsibilities, tasks, and status of lay missionaries are still different from those of religious personnel. In the future these distinctions will become less apparent and might disappear altogether.

In the past religious congregations abroad determined the places where they were going to work and decided on the personnel they were going to assign to that work. In the future the existence of national churches in developing countries will make religious congregations dependent on the requests from these national churches as well as on their priorities. In the past, mission stations, hospitals, schools, and other institutions depended on the resources from the homeland and from colonial administration, and they were modelled on those existing in the homeland. They paid little attention to local architecture and decorative patterns.

The church in traditional mission countries will have to make a contribution towards the building of the nation in the most varied fields: education, health, social structures, community formation, economic development, rural emancipation, human rights. This is the collective task of the whole community of which the church has to be part. Christianity has to be made part of the new era and that will require cooperation from the worldwide community of Christians. The nations of the world have established the United Nations with a view to maintaining peace and improving the living conditions of all the people of the world. The UN has a great number of specialized agencies for different fields of activity: the International Labour Organization for working conditions, employment, and social security; UN-

ESCO for education and science; the World Health Organization for health care; the FAO for agricultural promotion and food problems; the United Nations Development Programme for mutual aid and cooperation in matters of development. All these institutions are representative of the world community, and they cover many if not all aspects of the life of nations and individuals.

I expect that the churches, faced with a new situation, are bound to establish a kind of United Church Programme for Spiritual Development so as to coordinate human, financial, and organizational resources at the service of the gospel. There will be a need for many people, priests, religious, and lay, to be sent out within such a worldwide church program just as experts and volunteers are sent out for profane tasks. Future mission activity will have to make use of church-sponsored programs as well as of state or UN sponsored ones. UN experts or national experts sent to developing countries may be excellent missionaries. Therefore the church's apostolate at the international level should be greatly extended. Global, strategical thinking and action on missionary needs will develop; congregations will join resources and personnel to be put at the service of the churches in faraway lands. This global strategy will replace the fragmented, relatively improvised approach which has prevailed up to now. Religious congregations may take on new and more open structures allowing for the integration of lay groups associated with their apostolate. The castle type of convent may give way to a flexible, open community of men and women, lay and religious sharing a common spirituality.

A church, even a social system, cannot really take root unless it is firmly planted in the culture and the tradition of peoples. Thus theological thought, teaching, and expression, liturgical forms, and church structures will be much more diversified than is the case at present. All this is necessary so that the church of Christ may be present to assure the survival and the development of spiritual values and maintain a sufficient space for spirituality and religion in the civilization of the coming centuries. It is evident that churches will be much less clerical than they have been so far; the laity will take a more substantial part in action and responsibility.

Churches will also be less power-centered and more community-oriented. It is quite possible that the division of Christians, which is a centuries-old scandal, may subside under the pressure of circumstance. Maybe unity will first manifest itself in works of charity and justice, in support of the poor, in liberation of the oppressed, and theological reconciliation may follow. This is a great time to be alive! This is a great time for mission. This is a great time for new vocations. Just as the gospel raised expectations with the poor and the oppressed of Israel two thousand years ago, evangelizers, missionaries of today and tomorrow, have to announce a message of love and liberation and hope. In this way they will be the successors of the heroic missionaries of the past and will continue the great tradition of the Church along new paths.

PART THREE:
THE SPIRITUAL LIFE
OF THE MISSIONARY

16

MISSIONARY SPIRITUALITY

Walbert Bühlmann

With the discovery of the new world, missions were subdelegated by the Spanish and Portuguese crowns: the crowns were responsible, they sent missionaries, they paid for the fares, for the construction of houses, for churches. For the past one hundred years, however, the missions have been subdelegated to missionary institutes. The missionary institutes have had the full responsibility for their territory, they have had their *jus commissionis*. This situation has radically changed since Vatican Council II. At the council mission activity was brought back *in media Ecclesiae*, into the heart of the church. We have a very good document—*Ad Gentes*—but if we had only this document most priests and bishops and other people would say that it was for missionaries and institutes and they would not even read it. What is much more important is that we also have *Lumen Gentium*—the principal document of the Vatican Council. We have now, in *Lumen Gentium*, for the first time in church history, the expression that the church is by nature a missionary church.

From *Lumen Gentium* missionary spirituality entered practically all the other documents. The church now has missionary spirituality and mission commitment as an essential dimension. I think the sentence which says that the church is by nature a missionary church is a bomb which has not yet exploded in most countries but which should explode.

First I offer some reflections on what being a missionary church means for our older churches in Ireland, Switzerland, and Germany, and then, in the second part, what it means for the young churches. Here is the first idea. Theology has to be a missionary theology. In the past, theology had nothing to do with missions. You can test that by checking the famous manuals—Tanquery and any other manual of theology written before the Council. You don't find in them the dynamic that the church has to be open to the missions. In apologetics the church was proven to be a universal church, a Catholic church, and therefore must be everywhere. This was an argument of apologetics but not of spirituality. Now *Ad Gentes* states explicitly that missionary

Fr. Walbert Bühlmann is a Swiss member of the Capuchin Order and a former missionary in Tanzania. At present he is Capuchin Theology Mission Director based in Rome.

spirituality is not just a few complementary lectures given during theological study but that all theology is to be missionary-minded. That means it is not enough for a theological house of studies or a university to have a missionary or a specialist on missiology to give occasional lectures. No, *Ad Gentes* says it is imperative that the professor for dogmatics shall show that the church is by nature a missionary church, the professor of church history shall show that the church is always a missionary church, the professor of Scripture shall show that the church from the very beginning by the power of the Scripture is meant to be a missionary church.

In the past, our church was considered as an ark of salvation: save our souls, we preached in the past. This is a very egoistic conception of the church, and it is not at all the original meaning of the church. Our being in the church is not primarily for saving our souls; it is for being a sign to others. The church is no longer an ark of salvation, but a sign of salvation.

The church is always a church for the others, for the whole of humankind. Biblical vocation in the Old Testament, as well as in the New Testament, was always a vocation for a mission to others—not a personal privilege, or a special grace to save our own souls. The prophets in the Old Testament, Israel as a people, the apostles in the New Testament, Our Lady, Christ, the church, had vocations and always vocations for a mission. Therefore, to be baptized in the church is not so much in order to save my soul but to share in this essential mission. It is not only the pope who is the church, not only the bishop, not only the parish priest; the church is all of us. Everyone who is baptized has to share in this essential mission of the church to others. This mission is to be a sacrament, a sign of salvation for others.

About a year ago I was in Hamburg for a weekend at the Catholic Academy. Hamburg is a typically modern town, two million people, about 10 percent of them Catholics.Of the two hundred thousand Catholics about twenty thousand are practicing. These twenty thousand represent 1 percent of the town's population. Quite a lot of priests and sisters and others are dealing with this 1 percent of the town. I talked to those priests, religious, and lay people. If your problem is only to save this 1 percent, to satisfy the religious needs of this 1 percent by confession and sanctification and by saving their souls, then you may forget even this 1 percent. What is 1 percent to the 99 percent? The 1 percent has a real meaning only if it is a sign for the others. The others should be able to look on these groups as individuals and communities and ask: how is it that this group, these Christians, have another style of life? The Christians should be a question mark for the others and after the question mark an exclamation point, giving an answer. It was so at the very beginning of the Christian church. Outsiders looked on these Christians and asked: how is it they have another style of life? And they were attracted and baptized.

So I say we are really a group of people in the church, called out of paganism, baptized in the church, not so much for our own salvation but to be a sign for all the others.

Every baptized person, every Christian, has to be missionary-minded and missionary-committed. Today many lay people are also saying: We are missionaries; we have the right to be missionaries. Some lay people were asking the missionary institutes ten years ago: Can you accept lay people? Can we perhaps also be missionaries in your service? Today they no longer ask; they say: We are missionaries, we have the right and the duty to be missionaries. They go out for two years or for five years and on coming back they are convinced that they remain missionaries for their whole life. Even in the home church the missionary charism is not something like a stone, put in the heart of a man or woman, which he or she has to discover and shine up. Missionary charism means that the missionary vocation is a reaction, a response, a call—not something given or not given. A boy or a girl at the age of maturation, on becoming an adult Christian, comes to see the needs of the church—of the church in Ireland, of the church of Africa, of Asia—and say: I am ready to respond to this necessity, this need of the churches. So the missionary charism and missionary vocation are always relative to the situation, to the present reality. A hundred years ago the mission vocation was a career vocation to go, ecclesiastically speaking, into a no man's land. In Africa and Asia there were not yet churches, there were not yet Christian groups, so we needed strong men and women who dared to go out and build up a church out of nothing. Today the situation has radically changed and the mission vocation is a response to the local churches now erected in most countries.

Many false concepts are still linked with the term "missions"; many people still think in terms of missions to poor people and to sick people and pagans, to whom we have to go to help. We have to encourage them to overcome, what I would call, this ecclesiastical lack. It happens that many people in their consciences, or consciousnesses, are living twenty years behind the realities. They don't realize what has been happening in the world and in the church— new mentalities, new ideas in theology, in philosophy, new behavior of the young generation—and in all this we have to help each other to overcome our ecclesiastical lack.

If we look at church history we can say that the first millennium was under the leadership of the second church, the Western church, our church. It undertook all the missionary initiatives of the past five hundred years. Now the coming third millennium will be under the leadership of the third church. The new churches of Latin America, Africa, and Asia have not only numerically the majority but they will bring in new ideas, new inspirations, new cultures. The Second Vatican Council and the first three episcopal synods were stage-managed by Western bishops and Western theologians. The fourth synod of 1974 was clearly managed for the first time in church history by bishops and theologians of the third church. They brought in new ideas in inculturation, on local churches, on the theology of liberation. All these ideas come from Latin America, Africa, and Asia, and the pope, in *Evangelii Nuntiandi*, acknowledges this contribution of the bishops of the Third World. Because of the synod of 1974 we know that in the future these new churches will be inspiring the whole church.

This new understanding of mission reminds us that we are no longer the rich and the others are the poor, that we have to give to them and help them. Today there are churches all around the world and while we need more missionary help, the modern term for missionary help would be interecclesiastical service. There are churches everywhere but all these churches are in a *koinonia*—in communion. They have to give to each other and to receive from each other. Therefore I say, even if the missions have changed in local churches, even if local churches are founded, yet our mission commitment is going to continue on to a degree. These young churches still need our money, our missionaries, our ideas, but now the new concept is that we need also the inspiration of those churches. And this is the next point I want to develop— the idea of a reverse mission.

Reverse mission means we are no longer in a one-way system—that we are giving and the others are receiving. Today we are in this *koinonia*—the exchange of ideas, of theologies, of pastoral inspirations. Today every continental church, every national church, has the right and the duty and the inspiration, I hope, to develop some specific characteristics, some specific theological or pastoral initiatives for their own situation, as a response to their concrete situation. But having developed such ideas, such theologies, and such pastoral initiatives, they will later on exchange these experiences with other churches. We are already in such an exchange of giving and receiving; this process has already begun. For the past five to ten years we have been receiving from Latin America the idea and experience of basic communities —groups of Christians, of laypeople, and not just the clergy. I would say thanks to God they had not enough priests; they were forced by this lack to take seriously the new theology of the people of God, of Vatican Council II. Those of us in countries like Italy, like Ireland, have greater difficulty than the Latin Americans in taking seriously the new theology of the church, that is, the church as the people of God.

We are still too clerical. For centuries we were a clerical church, and it is hard to change such a mentality in Italy or in Ireland. In Africa and in Latin America this theology of the people of God was developed in these basic communities, quickly and radically. And so we are now receiving from them their experience of spontaneity in liturgy. I was in Kinshasa a year ago and in a very busy bush station I saw the Zaire liturgy: the church full of people, children and adults sharing two hours in a dramatic, real celebration, singing and raising hands and saying our "Father in Heaven." This is spontaneity. I think we are at the beginning of new possibilities in liturgy and we can receive a lot from Africa.

From Asia we are receiving the technique of meditation. It is done mostly outside of the church. In towns like London, Paris, and in all the big towns of Germany we have centers of yoga and meditation. There are lots of such centers in the United States. In Germany and Switzerland there are several monasteries of men and women who follow such courses, who practice this Asian meditation in their own communities, and who are giving courses for local laypeople on transcendental meditation, on yoga, zen, and so on. Cardinal Danielou said twenty years ago in one of his books, "from Africa we shall receive a renewal of our liturgy: from Asia we will receive a renewal of our meditation."

We have from the United States church the Catholic Charismatic renewal. It began about ten years ago in the United States as a Catholic movement, was first approved (to the surprise of many people) by the bishops there, and from there it has come to all Western countries. A second contribution of the United States church will be in the area of women's ministry in the church. There are very involved and committed sisters and laywomen who have this desire to serve in the ministry and it is their right to ask that women be no longer discriminated against in the church.

So you see, in this exchange from one continent to another, from one country to another, we really become a Catholic church, a rich church, a pluriform church, and a living church, a church in *koinonia*, in communion.

I would like to speak briefly about the young churches. It has been said that the response of the young churches to mission commitment is a new fact. Vatican Council II, in *Ad Gentes* 20, said that every local church, as part of the universal church, has to be by nature a missionary church. This was a new idea. These churches, which were called mission churches, have since become active missionary churches. They have developed their own initiatives, perhaps the priests less than the laypeople. Among the laypeople we have basic communities in Latin America, Africa, and Asia. We have people who are very committed to their church and to expanding the church. In many of these young countries there are mission institutes for priests.

We still need to send missionaries but not at the same rates as we did in the good old days. Therefore I say that today's missionary crisis is a time of reflection; we have to deepen our commitment, to be realistic. I say these new young churches still need cooperation, they need missionaries, but not to the same extent they did in the past. As a whole I think the church is more missionary-minded and active than ever. It is not a matter of having a monopoly, but of being an active part in the whole church.

Spirituality is not so much a system of doctrines or of theories as it is the behavior of every Christian to be open to the Spirit, as St. Paul was open to the Spirit. We were taught in the past that St. Paul was a great missionary, a great intelligent man who had his plan like the general of an army and said, I have to go there, and there and there, converting and traversing the whole world. But this was not so. In Acts 16 we read that he had a plan to go from Troas back into Asia but he said twice that the Spirit prevented it, the Spirit did not allow it. And instead of going back to Asia he went to Macedonia, to Greece, to Rome, and remained there because he had been open to the Spirit. That means he had read the signs of the times in the light of the Spirit, in the inspiration of the Spirit. Therefore, the church has become, providentially, a

Western church and now, in our generation, it has finally become a church of six continents.

Inspiration of the Spirit, therefore, is not just something static which happened in the old days when the evangelists wrote the Gospels, that they had for that time only and that we no longer have today. I am convinced that the Spirit continues to work in all of us. Having spiritual inspiration is a matter of being open to the Spirit. We must tell that to everybody so that the church becomes a missionary church by nature and through Christ. This should lead to practical applications so that the Gospel is preached to everybody. The church has to be a sign of salvation for all.

17

A MISSIONARY REFLECTION FROM ST. JOHN

John Quinlan

Our reflection takes the form of three questions:
1. What is the nature and purpose of John 21:1–14?
2. What message has the passage for us?
3. What does the passage tell us *now* about our missionary conviction and motivation?

THE NATURE AND PURPOSE OF JOHN 21

A commentator says that chapter 21 of John's Gospel "bristles with so many problems that it is almost impossible to say anything valuable about it in a short space." We agree without qualification. Here are some of these problems: Who was its author? How many distinct episodes have been knitted or tacked together? What is the relation of the first part (our passage) to the miraculous catch of fish in Luke 5:1–11? And there are others which can be added to that list: for example, having seen the risen Jesus in Jerusalem and having been commissioned as apostles (John 20), why would the disciples return to Galilee and aimlessly resume their ordinary occupations? And, having seen the risen Jesus twice, face to face, why would the disciples fail to recognize him when he appeared again? This is hardly the place to discuss these questions. Instead, we shall state as simply and as briefly as possible, the approach we adopt to enable us to reflect on our missionary conviction and motivation through the medium of John 21:1–14.

a. The Gospel of John clearly ends with chapter 20. With verse 30-31 the writer of the Gospel put down his pen. Chapter 21 then was not part of the original plan of the Gospel. It is an addition that is in the nature of an epilogue. As such, it takes up some of the themes of the Gospel (e.g., Peter's denial; the shepherd's care for the sheep; the role of the beloved disciple) and completes their lines of thought. It must have been included in the very ear-

Fr. John Quinlan, S.M.A., is lecturer in mission studies at St. Patrick's College, Maynooth, Ireland.

liest copies of the Gospel. No manuscript evidence testifies to its absence; the Gosple was never circulated without it.

b. This epilogue was probably added by a redactor, a Johannine disciple who "shared the same general world of thought as the evangelist, and who desired more to complete the Gospel than to change its impact."

c. In this epilogue the redactor has incorporated some ancient material which was not included in the "first edition" of the Gospel. That material (for reasons we need not enumerate here) include the story of Jesus' first post-resurrectional appearance to Peter. For this is what we believe we have here in chapter 21.

John 21, then, has preserved a memory of the appearance to Peter mentioned in the original catechesis in 1 Corinthians 15. He has given us a reasonably faithful form of that meeting, with some admixtures from another scene—the story of the first Galilean appearance of Jesus to the Twelve. It is from that story that the detail of the meal of bread and fish (and some others) come.

But so much for detective work. I give it in brief form simply as an aid to understanding some obvious "curiosities" in the text of chapter 21. Our concern here, however, is with the combined narrative which the author has given us in chapter 21. It has its own sequence and theological import. To that we now turn, specifically to verses 1–14.

THEOLOGICAL THEME RELEVANT
TO OUR MISSIONARY CONVICTION AND MOTIVATION

The risen Jesus reveals himself to the seven during a fishing scene. It appears that after the death of Jesus, Peter and the others returned to the occupation they knew best. The fishing expedition proved unsuccessful. Without Jesus, the author seems to be saying, they can do nothing (John 15:5). It is at this low point in their fortunes that the risen Jesus comes to reveal himself. The marvelous catch of fish occasions recognition of the risen Lord. What is immediately striking about this scene is that the initiative lies with the risen Lord. His presence and power give direction and meaning to the hitherto fruitless work of the disciples. It is, however, when they hear and obey his work, and let their net down to starboard, that the abundant catch of fish—a recognized sign of God's favor—results. The risen Lord seems to need their cooperation before he can reveal himself.

And then there is the import of the catch of fish. That seems to be twofold. First, it leads to recognition of the risen Lord. John it is who recognizes him. Clearly the more a person loves, the more perceptive he or she becomes. Peter is the first to act—he was a man of great generosity of heart. This recognition, however, is not a once-and-for-all act. The seven still remain somewhat puzzled and unsure. Witness the second hesitating recognition in verse 12: "None of the disciples was bold enough to ask, Who are you? They knew quite well it was the Lord." The mystery of the presence and power of that risen Lord was something they would have to keep working at. For the kind of recognition envisaged here is not the superficial recognition of someone who has been away for a week or two. It is something much deeper and more mysterious. It is, in fact, the recognition of faith. And so it can be at once an immediate and slow and recurring process. Christ needs to be "seen" over and over again—in people as well as in events before he can effect what he wants in us. For, as someone put it, the decision of faith is never final; it needs constant renewal in every fresh situation.

Second, the catch of fish is a vehicle of symbolism (a fact which does not surprise us in John's Gospel). It symbolizes the apostolic mission which will "catch men." In Johannine thought the resurrection belongs to the process of lifting up Jesus to the Father. When this is done, Jesus will draw all people to himself (John 12:31: "When I am lifted up from the earth, I shall draw all men to myself"). The risen Jesus fullfils this prophecy through the apostolic ministry, here symbolized by the catch of fish and its hauling ashore.

It has been correctly noted that there are no words of apostolic mission in John 21:1-14—an essential feature of post-resurrectional appearances to the disciples. The symbolism that surrounds the catch of fish supplies this element of mission. One writer says: "It is not too great an exaggeration to say that the catch of fish is the dramatic equivalent of the command given in the Matthean account of Galilean appearance: 'Go, therefore, and make disciples of all nations' (28:19)." And the symbolism has been teased out by the author. He notes that the catch numbered 153 fish—a number which Saint Jerome said was the total of the kinds of fish known to Greek zoologists. Be that as it may, the number for the author clearly highlights the breadth or universality of the Christian mission. It has an all-embracing character—the Christian community can embrace people of every kind, of every race, color, or character. Further, the net remains unbroken ("In spite of there being so many the net was not broken," v. 11) indicating that the Christian community is "not rent by schism, despite the great numbers and different kinds of people brought into it." There is room for all; and each person and nation has its own contribution to make towards understanding the full implications of the Good News of the Gospel.

So this composite scene from John 21 states and preserves the basic message common to the other appearances to the disciples: Jesus is truly risen and has been seen by witnesses who, in turn, have been sent to proclaim him to all people.

One of the stories that originally lies behind John 21:1-14 is that of a meal of bread and fish offered by Jesus to his disciples, which led them to recognize him as the risen Lord. An element of this story is still found in v. 12, but it is attenuated by the fact that a recognition of Jesus by the beloved disciple and Peter is recorded in v. 7.

We cannot discover whether the meal was an actual Eucharist or not. The question is whether the meal has taken on a sacramental symbolism and become evocative of the Eucharist. "To what extent was the description of the meal meant to remind the reader of the Eucharist, and cause him to associate the Eucharist with the presence of the risen Christ in the Christian community?" (Brown).

There are good reasons for finding eucharistic symbolism in the meal:

a. The description of the meal in v. 13—Jesus "took the bread and gave it to them and did the same with the fish"—echoes the description of the meal eaten after the multiplication of the loaves and fish in 6:11: "Jesus took the loaves of bread, gave thanks, and passed them around to those sitting there; and he did the same with the fish."

b. The scenes in chapter 6 and 21 are the only ones in the fourth Gospel to occur by the Sea of Tiberias. This naturally helps the reader to make a connection between the two meals.

c. In all the Gospels the account of the multiplication meal has been conformed to the account of the actions of Jesus at the Last Supper. The result is that a connection was made between the multiplication meal and the Last Supper. In John's account of the multiplication meal there are several details evocative of the Eucharist.

We doubt then that a meal so similar to the multiplication meal could be described in John 21 without reminding the Johannine community of the Eucharist. They would find their risen Jesus in the breaking of bread. Eucharistic symbolism is plausible then. Thus the risen Jesus in John 21 plays somewhat the same role he played in chapter 20. In 20:19-23 he was the dispenser of gifts, especially of the Spirit, the source of eternal life. Here in chapter 21 the risen Jesus also dispenses life: "The bread that I shall give is my own flesh for the life of the world" (6:5).

WHAT DOES JOHN 21:1-14 TELL US
ABOUT OUR MISSIONARY CONVICTION AND MOTIVATION?

a. The first and most important lesson the author of these verses would have us learn and take to heart as well as to mind is that the lordship of Jesus is central to Christianity. If this is so, then missionary activity is simply "the honest and necessary response." One of America's leading theologians touched on the necessity of this absolutely primary confession of the Christian faith. Carl Braaten said:

> In the present time the established churches are retreating from their world missionary dreams, doubled over with cramps of guilt and of doubt concerning their colonial image in the Third World. Theology of mission is in a state of confusion. It has become completely tongue-tied and, even more, in face of the resurgence of vitality in the non-Christian religions. The one result is a tendency for Christianity to think of itself

as one religion among the pluralism of religions and settle for something like co-existence. . . . The effect of this is to co-opt into Christianity all the morally elite of the world's religions wholly apart from the confession of Jesus as Lord.

We are called first and foremost to a conscious witness to the reality of the lordship of Jesus. If that is in any way watered down or weakened then our Christian mission flounders. Saint Paul puts it well:

> Even though there are so-called gods in the heavens and on earth—there are, to be sure, many such gods and lords—for us there is one God, the Father from whom all things come and for whom we live; and one Lord Jesus Christ, through whom everything was made and through whom we live (1 Cor. 8:5–6).

To confess Jesus as Lord is another way of saying, "I believe in his resurrection." And so the resurrecton is inescapably central to Christianity. It was because of its faith in the risen Jesus that the young Christian church made the step from recognizing Jesus as a wonder-worker and preacher of the kingdom to a confession of his cosmic lordship. It was because Jesus was raised from the dead by the Father that what he had done on earth was consummated in glory, and that all possible restrictions on his lordship were lifted. So it was that the resurrection was not a historical event in the ordinary sense of the word. It had to transcend history if Jesus' lordship was to transcend historical time, if it was to be a lordship for all time and for all people. And if Jesus is Lord, then the world just isn't the same as it was before he began exercising lordship.

b. We Christians then find our identity through our relationship to the Lord Jesus Christ. And that identity involves being a missionary. This too is inescapably central to Christianity. I sometimes wonder if we realize this fully. The Gospels leave us in no doubt. All four end with an appearance of the risen Lord sending the apostles on their mission. It is striking that all four Gospels should conclude in this way. The implication of this is clear. "It means that, in the traditions underlying the resurrection accounts and in all the churches which carried these traditions, it was understood that the ultimate significance of the resurrection was to be found in the apostolic mission." The significance of this is that the seeing of the risen Lord and mission are bound up together from the very outset. It is not that the apostles first met the risen Jesus and, reflecting on the consequences of what they had seen, came to the conclusion that they had to preach the gospel. Mission was not a theological conclusion added to faith in the resurrection of Jesus. "It was the resurrection itself which was perceived as mission." Probably Matthew gets it all together in the proper perspective. For he constructs his resurrection accounts in a way that the missionary mandate seems to have been given on the very day of the resurrection itself, also as if there had hardly been any other appearance of the risen Lord.

> Whatever may be its historical value, this striking abridgement brings out forcefully what Paul also says in 1 Cor. 9:1: "Have I not seen Jesus our Lord? Am I not an apostle?"The very experience of "seeing" the Lord cast him as an apostle. Seeing and being sent were perceived as one in the same apprehension of faith [Legrand, *Good News and Witness,* p. 53].

So it is for all of us Christians too. So it was for Paul when he looked back upon his life; he could trace the compulsion he felt in himself to announce the Good News to that moment of enlightenment on the road to Damascus.

So it was for the seven men in that boat on the Lake of Tiberias. That miraculous haul of fish opened their eyes to the presence of their risen Lord and to the apostolic mission that they were called to undertake. It probably took them a fairly long process of hesitations, tensions, attempts, and withdrawals to discover all the implications of that meeting. But at the end of it what emerged was the explicit clarity of the missionary command in Matthew 28:19. And that missionary command expressed the meaning of that meeting by the Lake of Tiberias. "The post-Paschal encounter with Christ was experienced as a mission by the witnesses—because in it they perceived that the message preached to the poor by the prophet of Nazareth was indeed the Good News of God" for all people everywhere.

So it is for us too. Our confession that Jesus is Lord is not just an interesting piece of speculation for some elite group of philosophers or theologians. It is something very real and relevant for our own lives and for all people everywhere. Faith in the risen Lord is not a precious treasure to be gathered inwards for oneself. It is, in fact, a faith that necessarily "scatters" the self outwards towards others. It has been well said that "a man cannot conclude from the fact that he is a convinced Christian that he ought to work for the missions. . . . It is rather that his Christian convictions are wanting if he is not actively interested in the mission of the church."

c. As we strive to come to terms with a new missionary era, it is, I think, our faith in the lordship of the risen Christ that we have to renew. Some think that we have reached a nadir in missionary activity. That, if true, should give us hope. I believe that our original option of faith is being tested now. I also believe that faith grows more in times of testing than in times of success. And it was precisely when the seven men in that boat had reached the nadir in their night's fishing that the risen Lord came to them, bringing new vision and new hope because of his presence and power. In the wake of Vatican II we have become more aware than before of how much we were supported in the past by structures and tangible success in missionary work. Both were imposing, and perhaps we thought our faith was great, splended, and invulnerable. But now we find it is timid and somewhat shivering. That is, I think, what we are experiencing now—the shivering of our faith. And yet, the witness we are called to give the world today is primarily a witness of faith. I know our witness to the church and to the world should be a witness of love. But, firstly and radically, it is a witness of faith. We need something of the spirit of John's "outburst" and Peter's headlong leap that we have seen in that passage from John 21.

Norton Long, the political scientist, describes the top executive of a city, state, or nation as an "uncertainty absorber." Major important decisions of any organization involve imponderables and cannot usually be based on demonstrable certainties. Accordingly, the task of the leader of the organization, because he or she has a clear vision of the organization's goals, is to radiate the confidence and optimism necessary to sustain the organization through times of doubt and uncertainty. I think we missionaries are the "uncertainty absorbers" of the church at the present time. Our lives and our work should be reason for hope and confidence in the Christian message. For that we need faith—continuing and lasting—in the lordship of the risen Jesus. For we cannot be "uncertainty absorbers" by hiding the truth, or offering grounds for optimism that do not exist. We can do it only by offering vision and hope. And that will come only from faith.

d. In all of this we need to be patient, with ourselves and with God. The recognition of Christ in faith is a process, and a life-long one at that. It can also be a slow process. We are so prone to doubt; the light is so slow to come. We know God is present everywhere in all the people and events of life, but we don't see him. We almost always want him to manifest himself in a striking way. None of the seven apostles in the fishing scene recognized the risen Lord at once. Maybe they were too immersed in their sense of failure. By his opening words, "Have you caught nothing, lads?" Christ contacts them in their situation of frustration and disappointment. They listen to his words and throw out the net once more. By their docility they lay themselves open to his gifts and to his life-giving presence. Docility to the word of God opens up to us the truth of the designs of God.

We need practice, too, because the resurrection we believe in is the resurrection of a crucified Christ. We have been healed by his wounds. Easter is the overcoming of Christ's passion and death—not that we need no longer remember it. Rather it established them as a saving event. And so the cross of Christ becomes a symbol of hope for all people. It took the seven apostles some time to absorb all this. It takes us time too. For we who carry Christ's message of hope and love are not spared walking the way Jesus walked. And it was, after all, in the "language of the Cross" (1 Cor. 1:18) that Jesus gave its fullest form to his message. His resurrection proved that he had not misplaced his trust in the Father—God vindicated him and proved his cause to be true. So too it is with ourselves and our missionary task. If we seem to be experiencing a kind of "death" just now, we know that God's life-giving power will "raise" us and our cause up again. The issue of faith always is: is one right to trust God in spite of the apparent uselessness of it all? And so there is resurrection, and God's work will continue, not only because the innocent and virtuous must have their reward and that good must triumph, but because God must, and always will, have the last word.

CONCLUSIONS

Our reflection on that passage from John 21 gives birth to three motivating and consoling conclusions:

a. Our mission comes from the initiative of the risen Christ himself. It is his task that we continue. So we can count on his help to bring it to completion, in spite of our lack of vision, our failures and disappointments. He needs our cooperation in docility to his word.

b. It is our faith in the risen Lord that makes us missionaries. It is only to the extent that we maintain a deep, personal contact with him in our daily lives that we remain truly missionary. We cannot proclaim him well unless we know him. Let it never be said of us that we resemble the blind man—not the blind man of the Gospels, but the man born blind mentioned by the philosopher A.J. Ayer. Professor Ayer imagines this man being taught the meaning of the word "yellow." He is taught the physics governing the movement of light rays and their effect upon the eyes, so that he could pass an examination on the subject and even perhaps lecture on it! Yet this man could not really know the meaning of "yellow." His knowledge is far less than the unarticulated knowledge of a small child, or an uneducated person who can open his eyes and see a primrose. Until this blind man can open his eyes and see, his knowledge is not merely deficient; it is quite useless to him. It is, in fact, only of use to those who can see.

c. Once we know the risen Lord, we are, out of honesty and necessity, driven to tell his Good News, everywhere and to all. As Dr. Mortimer Arias said at the Fifth Assembly of the World Council of Churches in Nairobi: "The Gospel is like manna—it cannot be kept. If we do not share it, we lose it. If we do not use it, it goes stale. It has been given to us, like bread, for our daily use."

In this contribution of mine I feel like someone (and perhaps you do, too) who, after listening to fine oratory, spells out the alphabet. But I have no shame in doing this. If you get your alphabet wrong, some funny things can happen to your oratory. And anyway, if we are going through the "night" of our missionary commitment, it is more important than ever to hold on to our alphabet. And it is useful, too. For if night was the best time for fishing for those seven men in the boat, the "night" of our missionary task is, I think, the best time to fish anew for the designs of God in our times. That way we are more likely to meet anew him whose task we carry only, whose presence in power is with us, who searches us out more intensely than we do him, who desires that all people should come to the knowledge of his truth: our risen Lord.

18

FAITH—A PERSONAL ENCOUNTER

Finbarr Connolly

God is calling us in our day to try to rediscover our own faith, to try to look again at what the faith means to us on a personal level. We are asked today to look particularly at the significance of our own experience of faith and its quality because it is precisely in the quality of our own experience of faith that we become capable of being instruments in the hands of the spirit of God to breathe faith into others. When we do begin to talk about faith in the missionary context, there is a lovely passage of the Acts of the Apostles that springs at once to mind. When Peter and the other disciples began to preach constantly and widely, this question was asked by their hearers. "How can these men talk like that? They are unlearned and untrained." And then the Acts of the Apostles adds this beautiful sentence: "But then they remembered they had been with Jesus." Now I think there is a wealth of significance in that little passage from the Acts. You see, Peter and the others had no formal seminary training. They had no training for mission in the strict sense of the word, except, as the Acts of the Apostles sums it up so beautifully, "They were with Jesus."

This is the major point I would like to make. The heart of the missionary is shaped and formed by discipleship of the Lord. It is only insofar as we are with Jesus, only insofar as our own personal contact with Christ is the dominating influence in our lives, that we become capable of being sent. It is something we know, something we have known in theory all along. What we really need is some sort of confrontation with the practical significance of faith for ourselves. If we are trying to renew it, or at least, if we are trying to evaluate our own faith, to look hard at it, we really need something that goes away from the more pious reflection on Jesus and the way to follow him. So, in that context, read this sentence from St. John's Gospel, 8:31: "They were with Jesus." In this passage you will find a direct description of discipleship. Take it as a standard by which to evaluate the depth of your own discipleship—a standard by which you may be able to see to what extent the words of the Acts of the Apostles really apply effectively in your own lives.

Fr. Finbarr Connolly, C.Ss.R., a former missionary in India, is lecturer in pastoral theology at the Marianella Institute, Dublin.

This passage describing discipleship comes at the end of a rather long argument in St. John between Jesus and the teachers of the law and the Pharisees. St. John then records at the end of the argument, "As he was saying this many came to believe in him," and then, "to the Jews who believed in him, Jesus said: 'If you make my word your home, you will indeed be my disciples. You will learn the truth and the truth will make you free.' " It is that passage of St. John that I would like to put before you from the point of view of evaluation. This is discipleship, and it is discipleship precisely as described by our Lord. What do we find in it? First of all we notice that discipleship begins with belief. It seems to be one of the basic ideas of the gospel. Whenever a person would come to Jesus, or whenever a person would enter into discipleship, there would seem to be an initial step that that person must take. You don't drift into discipleship, you are not born into discipleship, you are not educated into discipleship. Where Jesus is concerned there is a starting point—a step, a moment, a confrontation. Interesting enough the faith that is mentioned in this passage seems to me to precede even the awareness of the truth. It is only later that Jesus said to the group he was talking to that "you will learn the truth." So somehow or other, when we now begin to talk about and evaluate faith, we are faced with this. There is a step which precedes even knowledge of the truth and it certainly precedes our adopting any pattern of moral or Christian behavior.

The level of faith is not on the level of our mind, nor the level of our behavior; it is on the level of person. Now what does it involve? Somehow or other the faith we are talking about now, the faith which is first of all a grace to ourselves before it becomes a grace from us to others, involves an awareness of Jesus Christ as alive, real, and part of our life today, and it involves a free decision, a step, to give Christ that place in our life at the moment. I think, in this matter of looking hard at the significance of faith, we should look to Jesus himself. We are not talking theologically, so we can use words with a little freedom. Jesus had faith in his Father and when you begin to talk now of your faith in Christ, your faith in Christ must be patterned on Christ's faith in his Father. So now listen to these words from St. John. "The one who sent me is truthful and it is what I have learned from him that I declare to the world. I do nothing of myself. What the Father has taught me is what I preach. He who sent me is with me and he has not left me to myself. I do always what pleases him." Now just look at the words Jesus used here. "What I have learned from him is what I declare to the world." "What the Father has taught me, is what I preach." When did the preaching take place? Possibly we are tempted to go back into the dim, dim mysteries of the Trinity or way back before the world began, to find the moment of teaching. Jesus here is talking about the experience of his own life as a life in which he was taught by the Father, in which he learned, and having learned, he preached. The picture given us is really of two persons, fully involved in each other's lives. To me that is what faith means; it is a step: conscious, free, adult. A step made in the complete consciousness of oneself as an individual human being. That consciousness of the incredible beauty and uniqueness and potentiality of one's own self.

Would you say to another, whom you called Jesus, and whom you know as Jesus, I want you to be in my life? It is a step. It is in the light of these words I now ask you. What is the quality of your faith? Have you taken the step? In that context, I can tell you of the experience that happened to me with a group of brothers in India. I was giving them a part of a two-year course on spirituality, and, after a number of weeks, we came in the logical order of things to the question of Christ: to faith in Christ, and particularly to the need for quality in our own faith in Christ if we are to continue our work for other people and to be renewed in the spirit of mission. And when I gave it to this group of brothers—there were about sixteen of them—they stopped me in the middle of the lecture and they said, "Father, stop! There is no need to go on." They said, "You are presuming now in the way your lecture is heading at the moment that we have taken this step and we better admit to you that we haven't. We suggest that instead of your lecturing us further on the topic of Christ, you allow us to think and you allow us to search within ourselves, either individually or together, on what Christ actually means to us." Have you ever stopped to think and ask yourself, how could I frame my faith in Christ? If I had to stand up before a group of people and say to them what Christ meant to me, in my own words now, not in somebody else's words, how would I put it?

There is a famous passage in the Gospel, where the dogmatic and institutional significance of the words often covers over the point I would like to make. Jesus asked his apostles, whom do men say I am? And they were very quick to tell him what people said about him. They say that you are Jeremiah; they say that you are one of the prophets; some of them say you are John the Baptist come back to life again. And then Jesus said to them. "But who do you say I am?" In other words, fine, thanks for telling me, you answered my question, now here comes the real one I wanted to ask you. Who do you say I am? What do I mean to you? Don't you give me now what other people have told you. Don't give me other people's opinion. What am I to you?

I think really that is what every Christian needs today, and we who are missionaries and priests need it more than anybody else. If we were asked what Christ means to us, we will immediately reach for the phrase that we might have picked up in a book, that somebody else wrote, or we will reach out for a definition that we got from somebody, or we'll go back to our catechism, or we'll go back possibly even to what we heard from our parents, our teachers. All of which are perfectly valid, but meaningless, until we are able to frame it in our own words, not born of any mere wish, but born of an actual experience of Christ. Until we come to that point, I don't think we can really evaluate or say it as we should. The policy of having every Christian go through a catechumenate is part of an overall African mission policy. This is the same point. There's a step, there's a moment, there's a confrontation in the matter of faith.

Could I again refer to religious life, religious training and seminary training? In religious formation do we ever try to provoke this step, this confrontation? Is that the key thing that we try to achieve in the formation either of priests or of religious? To me that is what faith means and it is in the light of that step, that discipleship, a step on a personal level to Jesus Christ, that one can evaluate faith.

Now let us, in the light of that, take up the other words that Jesus said, the words that he spoke to those who had not believed in him. "If you make my word your home, you will indeed be my disciples." After that initial step of faith, that initial confrontation with the Lord, we must, in his words, "make my words your home." What precisely does that idea convey? To remain in the word of Christ, to make our home in it, to be a listener by profession. A Christian disciple is essentially a listener, but a listener to a living God. Actually, if we take Christianity and place it among all the religions of the world we would naturally try at some stage or other to put our faith into a category. The fact that we believe that it is the true faith doesn't prevent us from doing some sort of comparative religious study. Every religion speaks of God and every religion seeks to put humankind in contact with God; at that level all religions go into the same category. But we can categorize religions very, very quickly when we begin to distinguish the way in which the contact with God is made. Some religions offer contact with God by a certain activity; other religions offer contact with God through penitential work and action. What kind of religion are we? Christian tradition is essentially a tradition of listening. The great prayer of the Jew in our Lord's day and up till now is the Shaema which begins: "Listen, Israel, the Lord your God is one God." In Isaiah, in the chapter on the suffering servant, we read: "The Lord has given me a disciple's ear, and he wakes me each morning to listen." So the essential quality of discipleship and the first practical quality of faith is listening.

This is a standard by which you can judge the penetration of faith into your life, a practical penetration of it. Could you call yourself a listening person? People often complain when lecturers talk about this idea of Christian listening, either to God or to one another. Especially in the context of our relationship with God people complain that they find this idea of listening with God to be empty. They say, "Of course I listen but I don't hear anything." I think the reason is because they are waiting for God to speak to them from outside their lives; they do not expect God to speak to them from where he really is with them, within life. The Christ whom we have to confront, the Christ to whom we have to commit ourselves, is standing before us at this moment of history essentially as the Christ of life. The incarnation is not just a fact that God was born as a child of the virgin Mary, not just a fact—it's a principle. When God wants to save, God moves in. God's word is spoken eternally now, eternally by human lips and a human tongue, in the person of Jesus Christ. Jesus is not somebody who came down from heaven and did a job and went back; Jesus is eternally God and man. There's a humanity like your own eternally in the divinity—eternally. Therefore, God is very much the God of life. To listen is to listen, then, to the actual situation of life, and the demands of life as it is around you, the ideas of the people you are working with, the insights of other people beside you, the voice of authority, it is in these things that are part of life that God speaks.

To be a disciple is to have developed a habit of listening and, therefore, to have developed an attitude of learning. As we see mission today, the mission-aries are by no means people who just go out to give to others what they themselves have experienced and what others do not have. That is not the scheme of things as God sees it. All are to be God's people, all. Missionaries today must go out as Christians themselves to the people they have been sent to, in a Christian attitude, as that of children: themselves receiving from God in whatever way God wants to make contact. Therefore, they must listen to the stirring of the word of God in the culture and the people for whom they work—listen and learn. To go out with a learning heart is basic to disciples. To think that to follow Christ is simply a matter of walking a path fixed long ago is to have a poor idea of discipleship.

Discipleship has to be creative. Discipleship is not merely following. We go in the very spirit that Christ himself had. You remember his words, "It is what my Father has taught me that I preach." Where did the Father teach him? Was it a sort of hotline direct to the Father each day? No, it was from the midst of life that he was taught. We see again, through the person of our blessed Lady, who taught Christ the things that were deep within his own person as a human being, the marvelous significance of the missionary. Jesus was fearless, a man of incredible courage and determination. Jesus stepped in always for the oppressed. Who taught him? Mary taught him. So who was the first liberation theologian? Mary. "He put down the mighty from their thrones and exalted the lowly": that was her mind, her mentality. She might have been a very, very humble woman in that sort of non-womanly context of that day, but within it she was that kind of person, who could in a marvelous way, by her own faith and vision, educate and draw out the potentiality of Jesus.

Jesus himself says to us, "If you make my word your home you will indeed be my disciples, you will learn the truth and the truth will make you free." Discipleship or faith in Christ is a process, it is an ongoing process, and the path of faith here, both for missionaries and the person for whom the mis-sionaries are sent, is a matter of learning the truth. It is remarkable how very often our Lord has associated himself with the truth. In answering Pilate's key question he replied, "For this I was born and for this I came into the world, to bear witness to the truth, and all of those who are on the side of the truth listen to my voice." Our Lord closed his life with the promise of the spirit, and although we today in our theological tradition are inclined to call the spirit the spirit of love, it is interesting to notice that Jesus always speaks of the spirit of truth, the spirit who would lead us into all truth. What is the truth that Jesus is talking about here? He talks of it as something into which we would be led, he talks of it as something that will gradually open itself out for us, and, interestingly enough, he never talks of it as truths, but as truth: a single, plain, simple thing, not a whole collection of facts, true as they may be. He talked about a single reality that lies behind all facts, one reality, just one. That gives meaning to everything else, and he said, "I am the truth." Jesus Christ himself is the living, moving revelation that God is love, that God loves us personally, on our own level as it were, and that God invites us to share this love with him and with each other. All of that is what we mean as "Christ," all of that. This I think is what Pope John Paul was on to when he talked of a missionary always preaching Christ; yes, but the whole Christ, the mystery of Christ. And the mystery of Christ is this: that in a man, a plain man, who is the son of Mary, God's message walks around. If you believe in this man and let him into your life you can share what is in him, the spirit in him that will draw all of us into one. That mystery, that whole thing, is what we call Christ, and it is the truth.

Are we people of the truth? In our society of today, if there is any little way by which we should see the quality of our witness to people, it is in this. Christians—convinced Christians—should be people of the truth, and disciples of Christ should revel in the truth. The place we work, the community we live in, should be a place of truth—a place where truth is welcomed, where people are absolutely free to say what they honestly think, without fear of being contradicted or blamed for what they are saying, where the truth of their feeling is welcomed—not a place where people have to hide what they think and hide what they feel.

How much of the truth have you let into yourself? Because this was our Lord's description of the disciples—you will learn the truth—you will learn it, it will come to you; you will be led by the spirit into the truth. How far have you gone? How much of a person of the truth are you? I think in this matter Jesus himself stands before us as a marvelous example, a person who never played any roles, who never covered up; he wasn't one kind of man for one situation and another kind of man for the other. He didn't love people for what they might become, but he loved people just for what they were. He was himself. He was angry. He was ironical. He was outspoken. He would even be contemptuous of Herod and call him a fox. Above all he was true—that was the one thing about Jesus, he was really true.

I think this is one of the practical consequences of real faith: we are true. We are what we are, we say what we think with love, and we are happy that other people do the same. One of the practical challenges of today on the level of the whole church is that the church must become more evidently a place of truth, a place where all facets of the truth are welcomed. The last statement of the Lord is, "You will learn the truth and the truth will make you free." The freedom that the Lord is speaking of here is freedom from fear and hopelessness. If faith has really come home to us there are no situations of life we can possibly meet that can absolutely get us down. Many of them will get us down far enough, but there is never a situation that is utterly hopeless and there is never anything of which we can be totally afraid because we have accepted the truth. And so to be free is to have hope, to have the absolute assurance that God is at work in our lives and God is bringing us what he did in Jesus Christ when he raised him from the dead.

A confrere of mine, in conversation about the resurrection, said: "I have no problems at all, none with the resurrection of Jesus, none, none; my trouble is to believe in my own resurrection." Yes, my trouble also is to believe that I will rise from the dead; my trouble is to believe that there is something going on in me that began in Jesus Christ, to believe that link. That is what the Lord is talking about; you will be free, you will have hope, you will have absolute certainty that whatever happens in your life, God is able to handle it because he was handed a dead body and he brought forth Jesus risen in the power of the spirit. That is what sets us free because it enables us to go to work with God, to go to work beside God in our own lives.

19

POVERTY IN THE CHURCH

José Comblin

At the Episcopal Conference in Medellín there was discussion on the subject "Poverty in the Church." The recent Conference at Puebla continued the same topic, the same theme, and confirmed the same commitment for the future. This commitment is basic to the pastoral apostolate of the church in Latin America.

The text of the bishops on this topic was divided into three parts: (1) The Situation, (2) The Principles, (3) The Pastoral Orientation.

THE SITUATION

For the church, poverty is both a problem and a challenge, and the very fact of accepting it as such was new. Before that there was no problem for the church. Poverty was seen either as a first option for religious or something that could be defined in economic terms. At Medellín, the bishops were talking about the reality of poverty. It was this reality which became for the bishops a problem and a challenge for the church.

The first point to be considered was that the clergy were rich and allied with the rich. On this point it was made clear that appearances were often confused with reality. However, there was that image of a rich church in Latin America: there were rectories, religious houses, and church buildings which were better, much better, than the houses of their neighbors, so that the overall impression given was that of being rich. Moreover, there was the might of the representatives of the church: bishops, priests, and religious appearing at public functions in the presence of the political and military leaders, thereby giving the impression that they were sharing power in society. In many circumstances the religious were hiding their real poverty, but were maintaining the impression that they belonged to the higher ruling classes. Such an image of a rich church proceeds from the idea that social prestige is a necessary element for evangelizing people—the idea that prestige is necessary for evangelization.

Fr. José Comblin is a priest of the diocese of Malines, Belgium, and professor of pastoral theology at the Universities of Talca, Chile, and Louvain, Belgium.

The second point to be considered was the system of taxes for supporting clergy and for maintaining church works. This system had become discredited and had led to erroneous opinions about the amounts of money received. However, not all these opinions were erroneous. I know of some cases—among the poorest of the poor—where the priest demanded two thousand sucres or about fifty pounds for saying Mass for a family on a feast day—much more than they could earn in a year. There was a reaction mainly from the middle class because they are more able to react than the poor who have not the psychological energy to react or defend their rights. To this has also been added an exaggerated secrecy regarding church finances. High school finances, parish and diocesan finances were all shrouded in a very mysterious atmosphere. The mystery of the financial situation of a diocese or a congregation was complete and total, and remains so to a large extent today. In most dioceses the bishop is the only one who knows the economic and financial situation and this secrecy can help sustain the "erroneous" opinions.

The reality of the situation, however, is that a great number of dioceses are very poor and an exceeding number of priests and religious live in complete deprivation and give themselves with complete abnegation to the service of the poor. The bishops said so at Medellín and at Puebla, but this fact escaped the appreciation of many; it is now being realized and is helping to erode the prevailing, distorted image of the rich church. The problem, however, is that, in some of the older parishes, priests and religious are not adopting conditions of the poor and are not living in a simple type of environment. There are many very poor dioceses whose bishops are poorer than the religious. The religious can call on international support, whereas the bishops have no such international relations to call upon. At the same time the bishops say and recognize that they, the bishops and priests of Latin America, have the necessities of life and a basic security. They live within the context of the poor—people who lack security and who have to struggle for survival amid anguish and anxiety. We have security and we have the necessities. But the great majority of the people have no security and few necessities so that poverty of the church and within the church is always relative. The poorest priest and the poorest religious are richer than the great majority of the people, and, if they live in a really poor context, they can still rely on other priests or religious who are in better circumstances.

There is even an international solidarity that priests and religious can rely on, something not available to the poor. So, among the Latin American people the wealth of the church is a scandal because we are rich for the most part. Priests and religious have middle-class standards of living—higher than the standard of living of the poor. The problem is that poverty is a permanent challenge and a permanent problem. We can try to be near the poor. Many religious congregations think they are making an option for poverty—religious poverty—but what is the meaning of this religious poverty when the majority of the religious are richer than the majority of the population?

There is another problem which was not discussed at Medellín. In recent years there has been in the church a neocolonialism just as there is in the economic and political order. This means that many dioceses, parishes, and religious congregations receive money and financial support from international missionary organizations and groups. In my diocese, for instance, I know that 80 percent of the budget of the diocese comes from foreign sources. I can say also that the great majority of Latin American dioceses owe their survival to foreign funds. This means that they grow into a state of permanent dependency in order to maintain a standard of living, a standard of pastoral activity and of pastoral institutions similar to the standards of the international churches of the developed world. There is a cosmopolitan model of the church which is being imitated more and more by the Latin American church. And as they do not have the local resources to match this model, they have to rely more and more on external support. I think the situation in Africa and Asia is very much the same. Many bishops have to make an annual pilgrimage to various stations, beginning with "St. Mark" —the great German Deutche mark. We are more and more building a church according to an international model, and the Latin American people cannot maintain such a church. This is a new problem.

This dependency on foreign money has another effect. Foreign money can create social works and socioeconomic enterprises so that bishops and priests are being converted into managers—managers of small enterprises involving foreign money. This new role is creating new relationships—patron to client—with the bishop becoming the distributor of jobs and of job opportunities. He becomes a patron and his people become dependent on him, and, of course, in Latin America and the Third World, jobs are so scarce and unemployment is so high that the greatest thing a bishop can give is employment. And thus the bishop, priest, and superior are concerned with giving jobs and employment. Unconsciously, and because he can rely on international resources, he can be transformed into a business manager. In my experience, a bishop, priest, or religious as a manager is an economic and financial disaster. If he accepts the role of patron, his clients come to make more and more demands and expect more and more from him. So he finds himself in many awkward situations. If, for example, his client is his brother or sister, why are there no jobs for them? The ecclesiastical enterprise or small cooperative is growing to the limits of international cooperation so that the bishop is condemned to make more and more pilgrimages with more and more stations—Frankfurt, Brussels, The Hague, Dublin.

The church is thereby creating a model of living higher than the local resources can afford. There is a holy conspiracy involved in that—between the upper and middle classes. In Latin America these classes do not want to help the poor. The church is seen as the enemy, and therefore will receive no help from those classes, and is consequently forced to rely on foreign resources. The poor are so poor that real collaboration between them and the other classes is impossible. The priest therefore in a parish cannot survive and maintain his middle-class status without seeking foreign resources, and that also becomes a permanent condition.

THE PRINCIPLES

It was said at Medellín that we must distinguish three concepts of poverty which have become traditional.

1. Poverty as the lack of the goods of this world necessary to live as human beings. That poverty is in itself bad and is to be rejected. This type of poverty is the usual condition of the great majority of the people in Latin America. The prophets denounced it as contrary to the will of the Lord, and it is most of the time a form of human injustice. It usually leads to violence.

2. Spiritual poverty is the second concept of poverty. It is symbolized by the poor of Yahweh. It consists in the attitude of being open to God, of hoping for everything from the Lord—an attitude of spiritual childhood.

3. The poverty of the commitment of one who assumes voluntarily and lovingly the conditions of the needy of this world in order to bear witness.

Thus there are three kinds of poverty: (1) the material conditions of misery, (2) the poverty which is that of opening up to the Lord, and (3) the commitment to the poor in order to liberate them from poverty. In this context the bishops said that the church is, first, related to the condition of poverty. The church denounces the lack of material goods, the conditions of misery, and the sin that is involved in this condition. There are pastoral consequences, because to denounce unjust conditions brings with it many consequences. Second, the church must itself be spiritually poor and live in an attitude of openness or trust in the Lord. Third, the church must be materially poor. The poverty of the church is, in effect, a constant factor in the history of salvation. The church must actually share the poverty of the poor and be committed voluntarily and spontaneously to the mission of the poor.

The bishops said that all members of the church are called to live in evangelical poverty, but not all in the same way. The poverty of the church and of its members in Latin America is to be a sign and a commitment: a sign of the inestimable value of the poor in the face of Yahweh, and an active commitment of solidarity with those who suffer. So poverty is not just a passive commitment, it is an active commitment to those who suffer. Such principles are very clear and have been theoretically adopted by the church. In practice, however, there are many difficulties, and these have become clearer and clearer since Medellín. There are economic, social, and cultural consequences. The church has, in the whole of society, a traditional role and a traditional image, and, by adopting this new attitude towards poverty, it is changing that tradition and the whole system of relationships within society.

This is provoking a tremendous reaction, which is in turn provoking many doubts and hesitations in bishops, priests, and religious. This is because such an attitude toward the poor—a desire to liberate them from injustice and poverty—is potentially conflict-laden. Psychologically and sociologically, bishops, priests, and religious were not trained or educated to handle situations of conflict or to live in conflict or to live in conflict situations. So for many of them, there is a crisis when they see their own attitudes provoking conflict. How is it possible, they ask, that my role, my traditional role of reconciliation and unity within the established system, of being a sign of reconciliation and healing, has now become one of provocation and conflict? The priest in his traditional role legitimized society and the established order, and when he perceives that his new attitude toward the poor is not shared by established society, that he is a cause of division and strife, then the problem becomes personalized and real for him. This is the crisis.

PASTORAL ORIENTATION

The first consequence from a pastoral point of view is the redistribution of resources and apostolic personnel in such a way that preference is given to the poor. In Latin America this was especially urgent. When I first went to Chile the whole clergy of Santiago was living in middle-class or upper-class neighborhoods. Schools and colleges were situated in these neighborhoods. Considering that Santiago has a population of four million people, three million of whom are poor or very poor, and that not a single priest or religious community lived in that poor sector, the question of redistribution of resources was very urgent. In the countryside, the majority of the peasants had not seen a nun in their whole lifetime, because all nuns lived in the cities running schools and hospitals which cared for middle-class people. Very often, moving from the city to the countryside, from the higher to the lower classes, was really a radical and traumatic experience for priests and religious. It was a new reality which began about twenty years ago, and it was quietly accelerated by Medellín. Of course it brought many kinds of opposition and resistance, because any movement of a priest or nun from the middle class to the lower class provoked protest from the middle class. They thought they had a right to the church; that the church was their possession; that the mission of the church was to be of service to them. And when the Jesuits in Mexico City closed their college, which was the finest and best in the city, it was a revelation for the higher and middle classes.

The Jesuits were denounced as communists and subversives. Thousands of letters of protest were sent to Rome. How is the pope tolerating such a thing, allowing the Jesuits to give up their evangelical mission, their traditional apostolate, allowing their service to be given to the devil? And so they protested, but of course the poor cannot protest; they are illiterate and not able to write; they cannot send letters to Rome. Congregations of religious, both priests and nuns, closed most of their schools and colleges and went to work in the countryside, in the shantytowns. This was a real revolution, a real movement, and was a direct consequence of Medellín. It has caused tremendous protests even among the congregations themselves, their Superiors General, and even from the Congregation for Religious in Rome. And of course the upper classes brought tremendous pressure to bear on all concerned. The apostolic nuncio in Mexico was inundated with letters—always letters denouncing, never approving, even when a priest was nominated to a rich parish. They would ignore that because they would think it so normal, so usual, so traditional. So the problem of redistribution of resources is not an easy one. It is a permanent struggle in any congregation of religious or diocese.

The second consequence of Medellín is solidarity with the poor wherein we make their problems, their struggles, and their anguish ours. This is a new reality, because in the past, the church made the struggle of only part of the population its own. But now it is different, the whole population is included. However, it is not easy, because it means a criticism of injustice and oppression, a highlighting of the struggle in unbearable situations which a poor person has to endure, a willingness to dialogue with the groups responsible for such unbearable situations in order to make them understand their obligations. And in 99 percent of the circumstances, these groups do not want to hear of obligations. In that sense the situation is very similar to that in South Africa, where whites cannot recognize that they have obligations. The rich classes cannot imagine that they have obligations; obligations are for others. The rich have all the privileges as a natural condition, and therefore to speak of obligations for them is unnatural. If a teacher or professor in a Catholic school or university speaks of such obligations he or she is immediately ousted. The director will receive complaints from maybe two hundred to three hundred families that this person is a subversive, a communist, an anarchist. And the attitude of the director will always be the same. So teaching social doctrine in a university in Latin America is impossible, totally impossible, because it incurs an immediate reaction from the families. They say we are at the disposal of the families, to educate their children. It is very difficult and provokes conflict among the priests and teachers themselves.

Supporting those who work with the poor is mainly the task of bishops and superiors. They receive letters of complaint daily about priests who are branded as subversives, communists. There is a permanent protest from the press, radio, and television against those who work for the poor in parishes and shantytowns.

The bishops have made the commitment. They wish houses and styles of living to be modest, clothing to be simple, and works and institutions to avoid all ostentation. Ostentation had been the traditional style. The bishops used to live in houses which were actually known as palaces, and even though these houses were not palaces in the traditional sense, the name "palace" smacked of ostentation, of association with the aristocracy. Now more and more bishops are leaving their "palaces," giving them over to social works, and living themselves in more modest conditions. This is important for the sake of availability to the poor. How can a poor man enter a palace? Contact with the poor demands a simple house. Helder Camara opens the door of his modest house himself. He does this every five minutes, but he insists on doing it himself, and even though 99 percent of the time visitors are there to beg, to ask for food, or help of some kind, he patiently does it himself. That is his style of life.

Another result of this commitment is the need for a new form of financial contribution not linked to the administration of the sacraments. The traditional method was always linked to the administration of the sacraments, and in rich parishes the work of the priests was always geared to the administration of the sacraments for the upper classes. It is not easy to change this, and not easy to have the change accepted by the priests themselves. It makes other kinds of spontaneous cooperation with the rich more difficult. Moreover, the workers are too poor. They may not even have jobs, and, if they have, they are very modest. Therefore they find it very difficult to contribute to *a degree* by giving in kind—fruit, vegetables—but in the cities, it is much more difficult. In actual practice many priests and religious rely on foreign contributions, and since 40 percent of all priests in Latin America are foreign, this solution is easier. After five centuries of Christianity it is not normal, but it does solve the problem.

Yet another result of the commitment of the bishops was the need to supply technical means to priests and religious which would be suited to the environment and allow them to be more at the disposal of the community. By "technical means" here is meant mainly transportation. Of course in Latin America, a car is considered a luxury, but for pastoral tasks, especially in the countryside it is indispensable—at least it is conceived as such by humankind at the end of the twentieth century. Of course it is very expensive to buy and maintain a car, and there is a question as to whether or not it puts priests more at the disposal of the community. It is adequate to the environment in this sense, but as a technical means it is a big problem. I think there is an analogy between the problems of technology within the church and those in society. Latin American countries are today assimilating the whole technology of modern society but such technology is relevant for 5 to 10 percent of its population.

The next result of commitment deals with the call to religious communities to share their goods with others, and to put at the disposal of the human community the buildings and instruments of their work. There are many communities in Latin America sharing their goods with others, and there is new hope in this area.

The next result concerns a change in mentality from an individualistic mentality to one of social concern and awareness for the common good. Living among the poor in modest houses unavoidably awakens this kind of mentality and brings a new solidarity with the poor. Human contact with the poor, with the workers, makes people more aware. Religious themselves have now become laborers. Fomerly they were not laborers. Nuns lived in convents situated, so to speak, on islands surrounded by seas which were more difficult to cross than real seas. Now in small communities, the houses are open and by opening the houses to human contact a new relationship is emerging— a relationship of neighbors.

These were the resolutions of the bishops; they justified a change and initiated some progress in the conditions of the Latin American church. To support the struggle, hopes, and expectations of the people is a permanent problem, but, in spite of all the conflicts involved, the church is becoming richer—spiritually richer.

The most Franciscan of the Franciscans is rich compared with the real condition of the people. We have to consider this also from the viewpoint of the poor people. I do not think they want a radical change in one step; for them the commitment is more important, real commitment to their cause and to their struggles. Poverty will proceed from such a commitment. The process in Latin America is not just the process of the Middle Ages, when poverty to a degree was good in itself, and when religious people were seeking for more poverty. The Franciscans sought more poverty as poverty, not as a social commitment. In Latin America the process is different.

The vocation to commitment, to solidarity, real solidarity with the cause of the poor, is provoking a poorer condtion. The consequence is sharing—sharing the condition of the poor. This applies also to a sharing of prestige and ostentation. The last thing a priest and a bishop is able to give up is prestige, social prestige. To cut off all relationship with the public authorities and not to be accepted in civil ceremonies—not to be beside General so and-so or the Chief of Police—is a deep frustration for them. Really few bishops and superiors in Latin America now accept that. I think there are two countries, Brazil and Uruguay, where the bishops consistently refuse to be beside the authorities. The authorities are condoning torture. When two years ago Brazil celebrated one hundred and fifty years of independence the bishops did not participate in the public ceremonies. They did not want to give the government such legitimation.

"We cannot participate, we cannot be present beside the generals and ministers of state, presidents of the Republic and so on for such a commemoration, for in our country, the situation is structurally unjust, structurally oppressive." Many of the bishops were not invited, of course. For many years Helder Camara was never invited—never—but others were invited and consistently refused to go. In other countries, in spite of all the good intentions, the clergy think that such prestige is necessary for the church and for the Gospel, that they should be numbered among the important persons in the country. Now, of course, for many, this is a clear sign of legitimation. They are expecting that; they are asking for that—will a bishop be present? For the poor people it is also a sign if the bishop is not present: they also are not there. So it is also a sign for them—poverty of the church is also poverty in prestige—social prestige, and that is heavier, harder than poverty in material goods. It is more difficult to be poor in social prestige than to be poor in material goods.

For us who are socially and traditionally linked with prestige—with the highest classes, with kings, presidents, the public authorities—it is something very difficult. It isn't only a symbol, although sometimes symbols are more valuable for us psychologically than concrete and material goods.

Sharing struggles may lead not only to lack of prestige, but to the opposite.

Three years ago three Chilean bishops were at a meeting where seventeen bishops were jailed in Ecuador, and after that the three Chilean bishops were received at the airport in Chile with a real form of persecution—actually attacked by the police, by representatives of the extreme rightest movements in the country. But, as part of the preparation for Puebla, we made a kind of investigation among the people and we asked, "For you, what was the most important event, the most important thing that happened last year?" And 70 percent of them answered, "The bishop was jailed." Our bishop was jailed. For them that was radical change. The bishop was always beside the police. But the bishop in prison—they had never heard of that. And that means for them that the bishop was one of them. Because jail, prison for poor people— that is a normal condition.

In the public prison of Santiago 50 percent of the prisoners are there without any charge. But because they are poor there is nobody to study or examine or plead their cause. They are there, and will have to stay there. Of course, when the prison is full, someday the director will expel them through anger, in order to accept another category. They were arrested, but how can they justify their condition? They are poor and the poor have no rights, so the fact that a bishop was jailed, was also a prisoner—though it was only one day—was a powerful symbol for them. It was a clear sign of poverty— poverty in prestige. A rich man never stays in a prison—never—there is always an important person to liberate him immediately, always an intervention by an important person. And when a bishop stayed thirty hours—there were international interventions of course—that was a clear sign that the prestige is not as important as before.

Well, that is poverty. Poverty because of participation in peoples' struggles, participation in their causes. That does not mean that everybody in Latin America is doing this. It is a minority, but there is a movement of liberation from ostentation, from prestige, from selfishness, from false reason, towards evangelization. We usually think that prestige, social status, "palace," and so on are good psychological means for evangelization. Psychological because people like them. It is a psychological means to observe social pressure, but not to communicate the real gospel, the real voice, the real message of Jesus Christ. Many traditional people admire the ostentation of the church, but have no evangelical faith. They are religious in one sense— they admire. They contemplate the ostentation of the church, the ostentation of the bishops, but they have no realization of the gospel of Jesus Christ and the message of Jesus Christ. They can be religious people, religious persons, but totally ignore the gospel of Jesus Christ. And this is the problem for Medellín and Puebla—the evangelization of Latin America.

PART FOUR:
THE CHALLENGE
OF JUSTICE

20

FROM DEVELOPMENT TO JUSTICE

Richard Quinn

In the 1960s development began to acquire many of the characteristics of a new religion, with its "heaven" being mass consumption, modern society; its grace being trade, aid, or industrialization; its saints the local entrepreneurs and technical assistants; its savior the five-year plan, or the World Bank. You could go on developing this analogy, but suffice it to say that central to the development dogma in the 1960s and the early 1970s was this view of the development process.

There were two important elements in this view. First, on the international level, development was essentially seen as filling a gap which existed between the rich and the poor nations. This word "gap" was an extremely important word of the sixties and the seventies. Various social and economic indicators were devised which would reflect the presence and the extent of the gap, such as literacy levels, mortality—especially infant mortality levels—life expectancy levels, ratio of patients to doctors, accessibility of clean water, savings ratios, rates of capital formation, ratios of imports to exports, and so on. From a comparison of these indicators it was possible to define targets and draw up programs aimed at reducing the inequalities. These were then coordinated, costed, and budgeted for.

Take for example the educational gap. If a particular less-developed country has only 10 percent of an age group in primary schools, and we are accustomed to thinking of 100 percent as being the right kind of number, the aim becomes, for instance, to double participation within a stated time. Thus one could deduce how many extra books, classrooms, desks, schools, and teachers would be needed, and how much it was all going to cost. From this it would be possible to present a plan to international donors and to solicit their help in meeting some of these targets.

That was largely the experience of the sixties—targets, plans, and budgets. The prevailing view was that of fillable gaps, and that these gaps were fillable through a process of international cooperation. The Pearson Report, *Partners in Development*, would be reasonably typical of this era, as would

Fr. Richard Quinn, C.S.Sp. is director of development studies at Kimmage Manor, Dublin.

145

most studies on aid and international cooperation, on investment in education, and so on.

The second major element in development theory at that time was the view of the development process internally, as opposed to the view of the process internationally as we have been talking of it up to now. Within less-developed countries, development was seen to take place through what was known as "trickle-down." That is, development activities, and in particular investment activities, would be concentrated in small receptive, modern sectors of the economy; from these sectors, growth and investment would gradually reach down to the traditional sector economy, would vitalize it, and, after a time-lapse, the whole economy would take off into self-sustaining growth. Rostow's famous *Stages of Growth* would be fairly typical of the writing of this period.

During the early 1970s, both the gap and "trickle-down" have come under increasing attack. Some writers, especially from Latin America, regard the whole notion of development as a smoke screen to divert attention from what is actually happening in the world. They see it as a paradigm substitute rather than a realistic model which helps understanding. Others would argue that in fact "trickle-down" has not happened and that rural people in less-developed countries are worse off now in real terms after more than two decades of development than they were before.

Gradually it came to be seen that however useful the theoretical insights were on a theoretical level, they were seriously out of touch with institutional reality. In short, the world that development theory described was not the real world which existed. The theory, to repeat slightly, had seen the gap that separated rich from poor as one to be filled through mechanisms of trade, technology transfer, and development finance. However, in doing so, it had ignored the ground rules which regulate the operation of these mechanisms. In attaching importance to trade as an engine of growth, it had extrapolated to the world at large the experience of Britain in the eighteenth and nineteenth centuries—but there were some difficulties accompanying the use of the analogy:

(a) The first was that since the relative importance of foreign trade varies from country to country, so the impact of a given export expansion could also be expected to vary. Exporting is much more important in some countries than in others. In Ireland, for instance, the export of farm goods is extremely important. If other countries don't have a surplus to export, no matter what export measures they take, it is not likely to benefit them. In very poor countries with little to export, expansion of foreign trade could be expected to be of marginal benefit only.

(b) Second, the theory failed to take account of the impact on less-developed countries of slower growth in the developed world with the consequent smaller demand for the products of less-developed countries. This concerns the changing capacity of exports to buy imports: put crudely, how many tons of cocoa will buy how many motor cars over time.

(c) Third, there is the whole argument about terms of trade, an argument

which is hotly debated. It is pointless to argue about the figures in detail because as one person comes out with a set of figures, someone else will come out with another set, saying if a different period of time had been used as a base, a different result would have been achieved; or that the cost of shipping, or the cost of insurance, had been ignored.

However, statistical niceties apart, there would be general agreement that, for many developing countries which depend heavily for their exports on a few commodities or raw materials, there are the following problems: the prices of these commodities fluctuate wildly; they have in general and over the long term failed to keep pace with the price rises of industrial goods purchased by the less-developed countries; commodities are the object of speculation which doesn't benefit the producer, nor for that matter, the consumer; if the goods have been processed within the producing country and are exported to a developed country, they are subjected to tariffs and quotas; they are subject to competition from synthetics. Now all that adds up to vulnerability.

Another institutional reality ignored by the theory has to do with the dominance of the multinational corporations. Much of the trade between less-developed countries and developed countries is handled by multinational corporations. Now these multinational corporations can be regarded as either the root of all evil or as powerful engines of economic efficiency and even of social progress. If you read a report by IBM, for example, on transnational enterprises or the multinational corporations, you would think you were reading about the Second Coming. In contrast, some reports from Latin America would indict them as the source of all evil.

What is clear, however, independent of whichever point of view you take, is that by their sheer power and size multinational corporations preempt some of the options of the developing countries. Exxon, General Motors, IT&T, Nestlé, and Unilever, are a good deal more powerful in terms of muscle—that is, gross annual sales for the companies, and gross national product for the countries—than many of the countries in which they operate, such as Tanzania, Zaire, Ivory Coast, Dahomey, and many others. For instance take Dahomey: Unilever operates there, and its gross sales are something like four times the gross national product of the country. So obviously, if those two entities are bargaining, the political entity is not the important one; in terms of economic muscle it is in fact the weaker.

Multinationals can dominate access to markets in the developed world. Three companies, for instance, control 68 percent of the banana market in the sixteen industrial countries. One firm controls 50 percent to 60 percent of the market in instant coffee in the eight biggest coffee consuming countries in Europe. That does not leave much room for maneuvering by a poor coffee- or banana-producing country. There are other aspects of power of multinational corporations and these lie in their ability to control patents and technology transfer. Payments from poor countries for these were estimated to be about two billion dollars for the year 1971.

The multinationals have great ability to repatriate profits, to attract local savings. If a multinational firm comes into a country they are able to mobilize local savings, though the fiction is that they bring savings with them. In fact multinational firms may raise 70 percent of their capital within the host country. They may repatriate something like 70 percent of their profits, as has been documented in some Latin American countries. And 70 percent of their investment comes from inside because the people who invest realize that if they invest their money in a multinational corporation they are not going to lose money; it is as simple as that. As a result, savings are scarce for local firms. Ireland and Canada are good examples.

Another disadvantage of multinationals, as far as host countries are concerned, is that they can create their own market by advertising. You have seen examples of that in such products as Nestlé's baby food, in pharmaceuticals, and in cigarettes. There is a definite advertising campaign to promote smoking in West Africa, even including air displays. It is also believed that brands that are being peddled there are the more dangerous brands—the ones that can't be sold because of government regulations in developed countries.

The multinationals also engage in transfer pricing. They can contribute to rural underdevelopment by attracting the able-bodied to urban areas in search of well-paying jobs. They use inappropriate, labor displacing capital and energy-intensive technology, and they also contribute to the international brain drain. There are figures from UN bodies which show that, in fact, the value of aid to poor countries is more than compensated for by the capital value of the reverse flows of intelligent, well-educated people to rich countries.

So much for the second institutional reality ignored by conventional wisdom. The first had to do with trade; the second with multinationals. The third is that sufficient attention has not been given to the whole area of aid for development. It was assumed that when rich countries said they would increase flows of aid to the poorer, development would, in fact, happen. Most people are reasonably familiar with the aid targets internationally agreed on in the 1960s. Each developed country was to contribute up to 1 percent of its GNP to the less-developed countries. Seven-tenths of this was to be of a concessional nature, and this has come to dominate discussions in aid. In 1978, the last year for which figures are available, only three countries—the Netherlands, Sweden, and Norway—had reached or exceeded this target. The most powerful countries—the United States, West Germany, and Japan—are not even halfway towards it. And as a percentage of rich country donor GNP, aid has hovered around .3 to .35 percent of the GNP since 1970. In other words, less than half of the agreed amount.

Other important aspects of aid flows should also be mentioned. These can perhaps be more important than dealing with the targetry. Whether people are or are not reaching their targets may be less important than the kind of aid that they are giving and the purposes for which it is given. There is no doubt that aid can be used to exert pressure on recipient countries. Aid can be tied to purchases in the donor country; it can be used to create openings for business interests. It can sometimes be inappropriate, consisting of aid for the export sector of the economy rather than for the subsistence sector. Zaire is an example of that. Zaire received a large amount of aid a number of years ago, but it was aid for the improvement of the ports and for internal transport—in other words, to facilitate the export of minerals. Zaire, in fact, has one of the lowest nutritional intakes in the world because it has very little aid for the subsistence farming community.

Aid could go, and it has gone in some East African countries, to a dairying project. Even this may not be as good as it appears at first sight. It depends on who is going to eat the beef, or who is going to drink the milk. If it is not going to be eaten or drunk by the local people it is really not of very much help. But the figures don't show us those kinds of things. We have to learn to ask the right kind of questions. The kind of aid given is probably at least as important as the amount.

In these three areas, then, the theory was out of touch with international reality: trade, multinationals and aid.

Equally, the theory was out of touch with internal reality and, as a result of the strategy, income disparities appear to have widened, while poverty, unemployment, underemployment, malnutrition, and hunger have become widespread. Growth undeniably has taken place, but development, in the sense of social progress, has not occurred. The reasons are complex. Some of them can be sought in the processes already referred to. They include the facility accorded to firms to repatriate profits freely rather than a requirement to invest them in the host economy, and the greater knowhow and bargaining power of big companies vis-à-vis small countries. But other reasons—and this is very important—must be sought within the recipient countries themselves.

Within society there can be a lack of structures capable of disseminating development throughout the country, structures such as roads, ports, telecommunications, banking and credit facilities. More important can be the initial unequal distribution within the society, particularly of such productive resources as land. So that if you intervene, as the West did, in a society in which distribution is heavily skewed in favor of a small section of the community, almost everything you do by a natural process will tend to exaggerate the existing situation. Because the society is uneven, everything in it tends to flow in an uneven kind of way.

Other reasons include the presence of a non-entrepreneurial, non-innovating elite anxious to hoard or to display wealth, or to put it into Swiss bank accounts; the propensity to import luxury goods; the desire of politicians to ensure perpetuity in office by expanding educational facilities, thus starving the country of funds for investment; the stagnation of agriculture by depriving it of the technical and financial inputs necessary to increase output; increased population growth. Expenditure on arms is also very important and is estimated worldwide as $400 billion in the last year, a tenth of which sum is estimated as sufficient to solve global food and water problems. Thus in many countries one sees islands of prosperity amid oceans of destitution and misery. Reflecting on this phenomenon, new voices, new theories, and new approaches have come to the fore.

Internationally, the kinds of changes suggested can be summed up in the initials NIEO—the New International Economic Order. It involves a recognition of the fact that in its heyday the present system did not work for the poor nations and will not do so now. The conclusion come to is that economic forces, left to themselves, will tend to reinforce the position of the rich. Thus, if the world is serious about improving the condition of the poor, the present economic system has to be deliberately restructured in order to bring that about. There are various areas in which concrete measures have to be taken. For instance, improving the terms of trade for commodity producers by measures to stabilize prices and revenues; control of multinational corporations; access by poor countries to the markets of the developed countries for their processed goods without their having to give reciprocal concessions; increased flows of concessional resources; the rescheduling of debt repayments of poor countries. (The total outstanding debts of the less-developed countries, it is estimated, will be $350 billion in 1985. They are over $200 billion now.)

These and related issues are discussed at four-yearly intervals at UNCTAD, where confrontations and rapprochements take place between OECD, the rich countries, and the Group of 77, the poor countries. Progress is slow. The agreements now signed seem like a distant cousin to those parented at the last UNCTAD Conference in Nairobi in 1976. For instance, a code of conduct for multinationals has been agreed upon, but it is not binding; the Common Fund is only a fraction of the amounts originally suggested.

Disenchantment with "trickle-down" has led to the popularity of a new strategy known as basic human needs, although there is some doubt as to whether this is a strategy universally popular with policymakers in less-developed countries or only in developed countries. Some people in less-developed countries regard this new strategy as an attempt to keep them permanently poor, and thus they are suspicious of it. The strategy involves defining development in terms of the basic human needs of the majority of the population for things such as food, clothing, housing, education, and, most importantly, participation. As such it represents the beginning, not the end, of the development process. It is only people who are fed and clothed and educated, and who are free to voice their opinion, who can demand the kinds of change which will transform their own society. Thus the basic human need strategy would seem to represent a step on the road from development to justice.

It is a step forward from the crippling disillusion and despair induced by the first two decades of development, but it is most definitely not an end in itself. It is part of a movement towards a more just world. But it must be emphasized that the human development of the people in less-developed countries is unlikely to be maintained for long merely by the kinds of changes summed up in the basic human needs strategy, unless these are accompanied by the long term structural changes described in the New International Economic Order. In other words, they are two parts of an approach—one without the other will be of little use. One is long-term, one is short-term, but they both must go together. If they don't, the chances are that better prices for raw materials will simply mean that rich people in poor countries benefit at the expense of poor people in rich countries. It is only long-term structural change that will assure poor countries of the resources necessary to implement basic human needs policies. The strategies are not competitive, but complementary.

The use of the word "justice" instead of "development cooperation" to describe relationships between rich and poor countries is more than a change in vocabulary or a change in fashion. The latter word implies a situation which is analyzed in terms of technical solutions; the former suggests a radical restructuring of access to world resources, and that is a highly significant move. In the late 1970s the world community began to be seen in terms of justice rather than in terms of technical solutions. Earlier, we talked about literacy rates and unemployment rates, and so on. These kinds of things were concentrated upon in the 1960s—strategies, plans, and programs to improve education, to improve health. Then these were costed and added up and that became a poor country's aid budget and the rich communities' targets.

When we use the word "justice" we have moved out of that, we have moved away from the domain of technical solutions. We are not saying that technical solutions may not be needed, but we are saying that technical solutions of themselves will never be enough. This is not just a move along a spectrum; it is a move upwards to a different plane, a whole qualitative kind of change. Therefore, in the title "From Development to Justice," more is implied than learning from the mistakes of the past. Our understanding of the problem has been altered radically, and a response which is qualitatively different is called for. It is no longer the crumbs from the rich man's table which are being scrambled for, but a place at that table which must be accorded.

21

THE NATIONAL SECURITY STATE

José Comblin

National security is one of the important topics of this period. From the Latin American viewpoint, we can divide the whole period after the Second World War into three periods, or three systems of ideas for representing the whole situation. In the 1950s we have the whole idea of development conceived by some sociologists and other specialists in human science. In the 1960s the ideas of that development representation became popular and were promulgated; they were finally expressed in the encyclical *Populorum Progessio*. Paul VI's encyclical was elaborated in the context of development ideology and development rhetoric. But in the 1960s another kind of representation was discovered because the development ideology did not respond to the real situation. It was not the real expression of the real challenges, the true challenges in Latin America and in the Third World. And, at least among the sociologists, development rhetoric was replaced by a liberation rhetoric— a liberation representation. The idea of liberation emerged from sociology.

In the 1970s the idea of liberation was popularized and adopted by the church, particularly in the Roman Synod of 1971 on Justice in the World. That ideology, that "justice language," that "justice rhetoric," was adopted by the church and by the many episcopal conferences after the conference of Medellín and recently by the pope in Mexico. But in the 1970s we were discovering that liberation rhetoric was not adjusted to the real situation. Our experience of the past ten years has been that liberation is impossible, that the obstacles to real independence, real liberation are so strong that a series of pre-conditions is necessary. And why is liberation impossible? Why were all our illusions of liberation destroyed in the last decade?

What is the obstacle, and what is the real representation, or the new representation, adjusted to the real circumstances? The immediate obstacle is the national security state and the whole international context that is supporting the national security state. We discovered in the 1970s that a real liberation is impossible without a new international economic order. The current situa-

Fr. José Comblin is a priest of the diocese of Malines, Belgium, and professor of pastoral theology at the Universities of Talca, Chile, and Louvain, Belgium.

tion in the world, a situation of permanent competition, permanent military, political, and economic war, makes impossible any kind of national liberation for the small countries in the world. Only big countries in the world may have some kind of independence, or access to a kind of independence: the United States, the Soviet Union, and China. And China is a half-independent state. So two and a half countries may be independent and the others cannot be because of the radical competition between the two superpowers, the two empires in this world. The national security state is not a specific creation of the Third World. It is a global framework emerging out of the Second World War involving the superpowers and transmitted since then to all the dependent nations. The structures, the framework, of the national security state, existed in the United States after the Second World War, even though it was not so evident. The American people themselves discovered the national security structure because of the Watergate affair. Watergate was a sort of Vietnam: the discovery point of the reality of the national security state and the reality of the American structure—the reality of an industrial military complex. Eisenhower had talked about that in his last speech, but nobody believed that there was in the United States such a machine, such a complex military and industrial structure. But after the collapse in Vietnam, after Watergate, there was a deeper consciousness and awareness in the United States that the national security was created in the United States. The dependent states of the Third World are, because of their weakness, corrupt in a deeper way.

In the United States there are some democratic elements resisting the Congress. To a degree they can resist. They can control the CIA to a degree, but in the weaker nations of the Third World, there is no possible control, there is no Congress, only a fiction Congress. So the corruption of the traditional democratic state is deeper than it is in the United States. But the framework is the same; the political machine and the political ideology are the same.

The American people appreciate their state from the viewpoint of the Constitution. They think that they are applying the Constitution and they understand the ideas of the founders of their country, but they are totally unaware of the real forces which are dominating their state and their condition. They totally ignore the fact that the whole political game, the whole political competition in the United States, is dominated by a small corps of big enterprises, of big corporations—a small group of troopers, a small group of leaders, who are always the same. All the secretaries of state in the United States since Eisenhower, or since Truman even, were nominated by the Rockefeller family, and all of them worked for Rockefeller: Kissinger belongs to the clan of Rockefeller, Cyrus Vance—all of them were nominated by Rockefeller, by the Chase Manhattan. But the major part of the American people ignore that totally, because there is a kind of resistance in the name of the traditional democratic spirit. And because on a local level, participation is possible. For all the secondary issues there is dialogue and democracy. For the military issues, the international issues, there is no dialogue. The American people never knew what was the matter in Vietnam, what was the meaning of Vietnam. For the important issues, there is no political system; but locally, for the secondary issues, there is democracy. Because of this Americans are led to believe they can democratically solve big issues.

Now in the Third World the situation is worse. There is no local political life. The political force is totally concentrated around the state. So the corruption of social and political life is deeper in the Third World; but the framework is the same. All the implements for the national security state system emanate from the United States to our world or from the Soviet Union in the Soviet Empire. So the national security state has been conceived, prepared, and is maintained in the First World. And the coup d'état necessary to establish it has been conceived, prepared, and carried out by people trained in the United States. All the military dictators in Latin America were trained in the United States. Their ideology is American. For fifteen years, since the foundation of the military schools for Americans in the Panama Canal Zone, more than 75,000 officers of the Latin American armed forces have been trained there. They received not only a military training, but also a political training. They learned there a political framework, a political system—the national security framework. And after that they had to seek an opportunity in their own countries to establish the new system and to adjust it to the local circumstances. There is some difference between a military junta in Uruguay, in Argentina, in Brazil, in Chile, but the political framework is the same.

And why such a system? It is such a system because security has become the first priority for all countries, and therefore all the development priorities, all the liberation priorities are subordinated to the requirements of security. Security: that is to say that all the nations are permanently mobilized. Before the Second World War there was a clear distinction between war periods and peace periods. After World War II there has been no difference, there is no distinction—it is always wartime. All the nations are in a permanent state of war, a permanent state of competition; the mobilization necessary in wartime is permanently necessary. We are permanently in a time of war, and the totalitarian form of a state necessary in wartime, usual in any wartime, is applied in the normal time.

The condition of permanent competition is just the condition for a permanent mobilization, a permanent balance of payments competition, and competition over scarce resources. So there are two forms of competition: economic competition and political competition. The competition is so intense that all the resources of the nations have to be mobilized in order to survive, economically and politically. All the nations have this priority: survival. Economic survival, military survival, and political survival mean total and radical competition.

All kinds of dialogue are in total collapse because of the national security state. There have been in this decade various international meetings about that theme. How is it possible to emerge from a condition of permanent competition? There have been many international conferences: north versus south; developed world versus underdeveloped world or so-called developing world. But all of them collapsed, totally, because the developed countries do not accept any change in the current economic structure. They refuse any kind of change, so there is no dialogue. This lack of dialogue is the reason why a national security state is unavoidable. The leaders cannot respond to the demands of the population. Development is impossible because of the competition, the radical and permanent competition and mobilization. We are in a state of permanent war in spite of all the speeches, in spite of all the ideology, because all the politicians, all the statesmen, and their representatives in our world know perfectly all the beautiful words about international cooperation, international aid for development, and so on. They know the dictionary of the beautiful words about cooperation, so their speeches are magnificent. And the speeches of the prime ministers and the presidents in the countries of the First World are really emotional. They know perfectly the vocabulary but the reality to this is nothing, nothing.

There is a deep root, a deep cause for the national security state, and therefore all the ideology of liberation is currently Utopian. Liberation is not possible: development is Utopian development. What is the first priority for the Brazilian government? The first priority is arms, an atom bomb. The second priority is their balance of payments. They have an international debt of more than $45 billion, so they have to pay $45 billion. How? They have to sell many things, and they have to produce for export, so exporting is a high priority. And export of what? Export of anything that is of interest in the American markets. Therefore they cannot produce food, health care, housing—only products for export.

Developing nations have to export also because they have to import oil. And to import this oil, they have to sell food. The United States needs more meat: well, we can produce meat in the Amazon region so we can produce meat for the United States, milk for the United States. The result is that in Brazil no poor people may give milk to their children. This is the basic structure of the national security state, and because the Brazilian people would not accept such a situation in a democratic state, because they would protest against such a condition, a dictatorship is unavoidable.

Without a deep transformation in the international economic order, dictatorship is necessary; it is an unavoidable condition. So all the campaigns for democracy and human rights in the Western countries are propaganda and ideology. Of course the Western leaders have not decided to apply such a rationale—that is for the ideological experts—but it is not to be applied and therefore in spite of all the human rights rhetoric, the real policy of Carter's government is not so much different from Kissinger's government or Ford's government. The language is radically different, the rhetoric is different, the words are different, but the reality is the same.

So the national security state is based on this idea: priority for war, competition—economic or military. In some periods there has been more stress on military competition; in other periods more on economic competition. Since 1974, the economic competition has been more intense than the military competition. However, both military and economic competition require permanent mobilization; they require a strong state, an authoritarian state, concentration of all the power in a few hands so that political parties really representative of the people are not possible.

In the United States, as in Europe, there are many ways of manipulating public opinion. In the Latin American countries, it is not so easy. The leaders in Latin America have not the same resources to manipulate public opinion, so in many circumstances, immediate repression is necessary—repression by the armed forces, by the police. Concentration of power and verticalism were created in the United States. An ideology of national security, a military ideology was created in the military schools of the United States. In the military schools, the military doctrine and the political doctrine are completely different from the traditional political doctrine of the United States. After Watergate, after the hearings of the Senate about Latin America, Americans were warned that in their own military schools they were preparing dictatorships—a political ideology for dictatorships. They became conscious that in the International Police Academy in Washington the torturers of Latin America were being trained. The Academy trained, for more than fifteen years, a whole generation of police in all the modern technology of torture. In the Third World very often technology enters into the nation that way—through the police. This is the first corps of the nation that receives modern technology—technology for interrogation and torture. All of them were trained in the United States, directly or indirectly. In Brazil more than one hundred thousand police officers were trained by American officers either in the United States itself or in Brazil (the Americans have police missions in order to train people in all the countries). Until recent years, the American people ignored that totally; they were unconscious of such facts. It was only after hearings in the American Congress that the revelations of such activities has provoked a crisis in the consciousness of the United States.

So we have a national security state: priority for security, competition, and therefore a strong state. A strong state, and a state where repression is one of the priorities. In most Latin American countries and, of course, mainly in the military dictatorships, the first power and the superpower of the nation is the secret service. The secret service is totally independent of any political control. They do not have to explain their behavior. The whole people is permanently conscious, permanently aware of the existence of the secret service, so that after ten years it is not necessary to intervene, to interfere—no, everybody knows that the secret service is present. When we are talking, the secret service is present. It is a natural condition and very efficient, because after a few years every person is creating in himself or herself a small police officer, an inner police officer, who controls permanently, constantly. The self-repression becomes stronger than the other repression, the official repression. There is an interiorization of the national security state. People are organizing and creating and maintaining in themselves their own national security state, their own system of repression, their system of control. And, of course, the higher classes are not conscious of that because they receive all the benefits—they are the spontaneous interpreters of the system. But in São Paulo a sociological study among the poor showed that more than 70 percent of the population think that at any moment they may be arrested. They are permanently living with the idea: "I may be arrested; I don't know why, but it is possible." After a few years the visible repression currently in Chile will not be necessary at all. The Latin American countries are integrated into the American system. They have to follow the laws of the American system, like the communist countries have to follow the laws of the Soviet system. They cannot allow any approach toward more independence; repression is the only immediate priority. They have to pay their debts: $45 billion in Brazil, $6 billion in Chile—they have to pay that as a matter of priority.

We all have responsibility for the national security states all over the world because of the lack of an international economic order. And it is the radical opposition to change in the developed countries that makes it so difficult, because for them the first priority is the status quo. It is maintaining everything as it is—no change, no transformation. There is radical opposition because of their own problems. In Germany and the United States the priority is their own problems, their own inflation, their own stagnation, their own unemployment, and the rest of the world may starve—it is not important. It is totally secondary. Because of that selfishness—radical selfishness—of the developed countries, who are opposed to any kind of real dialogue, the condition that makes the national security state necessary in the Third World remains. The goals are clear. The first goal is a real new economic order—a real economic collaboration in this world, collaboration within the Western system and throughout the whole world, collaboration between the two empires, and less competition between the two worlds. That seems an impossible task. Or is it possible to persuade the developed countries? In the developed countries the priority, the ideology, the aim is growth—economic growth. And just because material growth is a first priority in the developed world, all the other goals are abstract: the reality is their economic growth. How is it possible to explain that to the leaders and the political parties? How is it possible for a political party in Europe and in the United States to propose to directors, "sacrifice and collaboration with the Third World." They think it would provoke political collapse for them. The party that would propose such a program would be condemned to a political collapse; therefore real collaboration is not possible.

I think also that the churches—Catholic and Protestant—in the First World are too silent. It is very good to struggle, to denounce the torture in Latin America, and so on, but what system is behind it? Who is reporting on that system? The task of the churches is to denounce the real sins, the real causes, the real roots of such a system. And the real sins, the real causes, the real roots of such a system lie in the lack of a real will for collaboration. There is no decision, no willingness, to really collaborate. And if the churches remain silent, because they want to appear more agreeable, to avoid contradiction with the economic interests of Christian people, is that the task of the church—to be agreeable? Is it not the task of the church to denounce the reality, the real responsibility for the systems in the United States and in other countries? It is a task for many years, and a responsibility of the church. It is a political responsibility but also it is a prophetic responsibility. It is the task, it is the meaning of the testimony of the church.

22

THE SITUATION OF VIOLENCE

José Comblin

The bishops of Paraguay, in their declaration of 1976, said: "We believe that the violence born of the heartaches of a few is what provokes the protests of those who are rebellious." The first violence generates the second form of violence. The second form of violence, according to the expression of the Paraguayan bishops, is subversive—terrorism, armed violence, extremism. It is an illegitimate use of force for revolution, insurrection, and social change. They call that the terrorism of subversives. And violence attracts violence. When the answer to injustice reaches the streets, the authorities believe that it is their obligation to save public order or to reestablish it, even if they have to enforce it by harsh methods. So the second form of violence generates the third form of violence, i.e., the violence of repression, police repression, and the use of psychological, moral, and physcial torture.

The reports of Amnesty International and others are very clear concerning torture. The new fact of the last decades is that repression is not simply torture; it is a technological torture, a torture that is practiced with the aid of doctors, psychologists. In Chile, in Brazil, there are always doctors, psychologists, assisting the torturers. Because it is technological, it is also very complicated, and uses complicated machines, which have to be imported from the United States. Torture is now technological—that is the new reality. Brutality is traditional but technological torture is not. There is a national budget for it. It is foreseen that the nation has to buy the equipment in the United States, and that expenditure is officially and systematically planned and budgeted for. The whole nation is implicated in such a process: they can ignore it even if they know it, yet they are all of them paying for it—the taxes are contributing to such a practice. This torture cannot be explained wholly by the spontaneous brutality of policemen—it is systematic.

As for moral condemnation, the problem is that the persons who are using violence never accept that they are using violence. They call it a legitimate use of force. So violence is always a charge proceeding from the victims, but never from the authors, so there is never consensus about violence. Violence

Fr. José Comblin is a priest of the diocese of Malines, Belgium, and professor of pastoral theology at the Universities of Talca, Chile, and Louvain, Belgium.

is always denied; that there is systematic and technological torture is always denied by the authorities. The public authorities will never, of course, accept, and will never publicly recognize that it is a reality in the country. Violence in the real sense, as defined by the church, is always denied, because it is believed to be right. Nobody accepts that his or her use of violence is violence, so violence is always a condemnation proceeding from the "others." Any moral condemnation of violence as a principle never reaches its true destiny, because nobody ever accepts such a condemnation. They always say, well, our use of force is legitimate; it is not violence.

The question of violence is a difficult one, because, according to the authors of violence, there is no violence; only according to the victims is there violence. Everybody is in agreement in condemning violence as violence, in the religious sense, but a condemnation of violence in itself changes nothing. It is easy to condemn violence in principle; it is more complicated to say that here, in this case, there is really violence, that is to say, legitimate use of force or illegitimate use of force—that is a moral, difficult task.

In the past, in the national wars for independence, in the European national wars, the task was very easy. Every church always agreed with the government, so the war of the French army against the German army was a legitimate use of force except for the Germans—for the Germans it was illegitimate. For the German church the use of force was legitimate. It was really very difficult disassociating the opinion of the church from the opinion of the government of the established society. Now in the last decades, there is more and more in Latin America a feeling of independence; that is to say, we have not necessarily to accept the interpretation given by the established society, the established government. We understand that the position given by the established society may be wrong. It is not so easy to accept that. In the United States the change was provoked by the moral crisis invoked by the Vietnam War. At the end of the Vietnam War some sectors in the Protestant and Catholic church finally arrived at the conclusion that the interpretation given by the government was wrong, and that there was no legitimate use of violence in such cases, that the use of force was really violence and that it was illegitimate.

In our time there is a clearer distinction between the interpretation given by the government and that given by the church, but it is very difficult to disassociate and create a kind of consciousness, a new form of criticism, based on the facts themselves and not on the word of the governments. In Africa it is especially difficult to accept the interpretation given by the government. I knew something as a Belgian about the famous case in Burundi, when more than one hundred thousand people from one tribe were killed and the whole church remained totally, completely silent, without a word, because they figured it would have been impossible to disassociate themselves from the government, from public opinion. The church felt that it was totally impossible to disassociate itself from the government, because the spontaneous respect for the established power was so strong that it could not imagine another way of life. That was a normal reaction, because in the European countries it was also so. In the Second World War, the whole church, the whole European church could not disassociate its feeling from the feelings of the government—established government. What I am saying is that it looks as if the problem in Africa was the same as in Europe—that the condemnation of violence was in many cases nothing more than accepting the public defintion of violence given by the government. If the government defines this as being violence, the church can condemn it because the government has said so, and if the government says this is a legitimate use of force, the church can also declare it to be a legitimate use of force. But to disassociate the judgment of the church from the judgment of the government is, I think, a difficult challenge, but a specific challenge in our times. In the past very often the church was not interested in knowing what were the real causes, the real accusations, the real sources of such violence, in order to understand whether it was legitimate or illegitimate. It simply accepted the judgment of the government. But today we have to judge by ourselves, to know by ourselves whether there is legitimate use of violence in particular instances.

In the past the church condemned any kind of revolutionary movement until the victory of the revolutionary movement was accepted; in such cases violence was legitimate or illegitimate according to the victory. The only condition for being legitimate is victory; so in Latin America, before independence, the independence war was illegitimate and condemned by the bishops and by the church and by the pope. After the success of the independence war, of course the liberators were celebrated as the founders of the country, and recognized as good Catholics. In the time before the victory they were not good Catholics; it was only after the victory that they became good Catholics. To decide whether victory is sufficient as a criterion in order to appreciate whether a revolutionary movement is legitimate or not is also a new challenge for the church. We have to give Christian people who have to participate in violence other criteria, and not only the criterion of the final victory.

There is also the question of nonviolence. Nonviolence is a series of methods; it covers dozens of specific methods of protest: noncooperation and nonintervention, mainly in the Anglo-Saxon countries, because there is more tolerance and a more democratic way of life in those countries. But outside the democratic countries, such nonviolent methods are very difficult to apply. The reasons are that those governments cannot tolerate such nonviolent protest. A hunger strike in an undemocratic country is very, very difficult. Any strike in Chile, any kind of strike is prohibited, so such nonviolent methods are immediately transformed into violent methods, and there is an immediate consequence. The problem is that by accepting and adopting nonviolent methods, we are immediately led to situations of violence, and therefore in the context of a nondemocratic country, nonviolent methods have to be created which will not lead to violence. Other kinds, new kinds, of nonviolent methods, though not the same methods, apply in the United States. Such methods are only possible in the conflict between the developed countries and the nondeveloped countries. Many people are more conscious that the solution has to be found in the United States. Public opinion in the United States is the ultimate factor that can organize change. This is also true to a degree in the European coutries. It is not probable that the European countries or the United States will accept justice— international justice—rationally and by persuasion; so the problem is what kind of pressure, what kind of collaboration of small Christian minorities in the dominating countries will be necessary to help the organization of nonviolent action, and change the mentality and politics of the dominating classes. That will be a problem for the future. What kind of nonviolent actions are to be prepared for the future in order to organize a clear demonstration, a clear protest, a clear peaceful protest? If we are not able to organize a peaceful protest and a peaceful manifestation, nonviolent manifestation, against the established order, violence will be unavoidable. A change in the international order and in the consciousness of the First World is absolutely necessary if we are to have peace and happiness for all.

23

LOVE OF GOD LEADS TO JUSTICE

Peter J. Butelezi

Saint Matthew in his Gospel says: "Take the plank out of your own eye first; then you will see clearly enough to take the splinter out of your brother's eye" (Matt. 7:3–5). In matters of justice it is easier to point an accusing finger at one's neighbor than to settle down and rectify an untenable situation in one's own life and situation. Were people, however, to engage in an exercise of mutual accusation and counteraccusation, then no progress would be made. All true reform starts with self-criticism and the putting of one's own house in order. We should face our failings with honesty and courage and try to do something about them. God will help us in our endeavors.

Working for justice implies working for those who cannot defend themselves or their rights. There are very strong religious motives for doing this. The defenseless are God's special favorites. In the Book of Proverbs it is said: "To oppress the poor is to insult their creator; to be kind to the needy is to honor him" (Prov. 14:31). Christ tells us that at the last judgment, he will say: "Insofar as you did this to one of the least of these brothers of mine you did it to me" (Matt. 25:40), and, "Insofar as you neglected to do this to one of the least of these, you neglected to do it to me" (Matt. 25:45). He identified himself with the needy.

God does not only love the poor in a special way and identify with them, but he also defends them and defends their cause. The Scriptures are clear on this point. Among various texts we can quote are, for instance, these:

Because a man is poor do not therefore cheat him, nor at the city gate oppress anybody in affliction, for Yahweh takes up their cause and extorts the life of their extortioners (Prov. 22:22–23).

Do not displace the ancient landmark or encroach on orphans' lands. For he who avenges them is strong and will take up their cause against you (Prov. 23:10–11).

Do not avert your eyes from the destitute, give no man occasion to curse you, for if a man curses in the bitterness of his soul, his maker will hear his imprecation (Sir. 4:5–6).

Peter J. Butelezi is archbishop of Bloemfontein, South Africa.

163

A general rule given by the Scriptures is that we should treat others the way we would like to be treated ourselves (Tob. 4:16; Matt. 7:12; 22:39–40).

Let us look at some of the problems foreign missionaries face. One concerns development. It is important that missionaries be involved in development; otherwise many people will see in them a paternalistic group all full of arrogance. Through involvement in development the foreign missionaries can help build up a whole nation.

Through the help of such foreign missionaries the local people would in time have their own leaders who will then plan and supervise the progress of the work.

It is all very well to say that the local church produces its own priests and religious. This cannot just happen of itself. It presupposes wise planning, patient understanding. St. James says in his letter that it does not help to say to a man feeling cold that he should get warm if you do not give him something to put on. Involvement in development is a proclamation that we have confidence in the people we work for and that we have come to serve.

It has been said that the Third World is not asking for aid but for trade. Translated into the field of missionary activity this would mean an exchange. We are all members of the same family, and we are called upon to share what we have. You give me what you have and I give you what I have and together we become richer. The very act of giving makes me richer. It is perhaps in this regard that we find a solution to that problem of people saying we do not want to engage in an ecclesiastical colonialism; we feel going out to foreign missions implies a superiority complex which we regret. The going out should be in a spirit of service. We offer what we have and what we highly value, and receive what the recipient offers in return. We all have much to learn from each other. The field is wide open.

One other source of difficulty for the foreign missionary is the very fact that he or she is a foreigner. People resent being told by a foreigner what they should do. It is an old story. We find it, for example, in the life of the prophet Amos who was told by the priest of the northern kingdom that he should go and preach in his own country in the south. Moreover people feel that the foreigners do not identify sufficiently with them; they feel that when the troubles come they will run away. They do not want to be left with the crying baby when the person who provoked the child is gone. Because of such considerations foreign missionaries find their situation often precarious. It is often difficult for them to gain entry, and, once inside, they are subject to expulsion at very short notice. This can tempt them to close their mouths. They are working under very difficult circumstances, especially in the field of justice.

All are agreed that their silence should not amount to a betrayal of their God. It should not be a counterwitness. They have to be on the alert so as not to distort their consciences. We also congratulate those missionaries who have adopted the country of their activity and taken up citizenship. It is often a difficult decision to make, but it is most welcome. By working for the poor and acknowledging their human dignity, we proclaim the great truths of the fellowship of all and the common parenthood of God. By showing esteem for those who have lost all sense of self-esteem we often win them back to the path of goodness. Here, often, the foreigners have an advantage. They can often be more objective and give disinterested service.

Many difficulties in the world today come because of a lack of communication. Often solutions come too late. It has been said of our part of the world that too little was given and too late. What is needed is vision about the future and boldness in finding solutions. Proper communications presuppose that the participants deal with each other as equals, trying to arrive at acceptable solutions and on time. This demands that all should be on the watch, especially when there are many difficulties of language and culture. This is a field that needs special attention.

In the whole question of working for justice it is important to give people a sense of hope. They have to feel that there is something that they can do and areas where they can help. Often people just see the task as impossible. There are many things that each can do and that would help. By working together to build a world in which justice reigns we shall ourselves grow in God's love. He tells us that "anyone who says I love God and hates his brother is a liar, since a man who does not love the brother that he can see cannot love God whom he has never seen" (1 John 4:20 f.).

Working for the poor is a religious duty to which we are all called. Working for the poor implies involvement in development work and in working for justice. These fields present special problems for our foreign missionaries: problems which affect future missionaries. We have considered possible solutions. All that remains for me to do is to thank, on behalf of those in the foreign lands, the missionaries, who for their Lord, have given their lives for the good of their fellow human beings.

PART FIVE:
MAKING THE CHURCH
INCARNATE

24

INCULTURATION

Parmananda Divarkar

The word "inculturation" does not occur in *Evangelii Nuntiandi,* so it might be worthwhile to say something about the origin of the word and about how it has entered into the missiological or ecclesiastical vocabulary. That will leads us on to the consideration of how to find these issues in *Evangelii Nuntiandi.* To the best of my knowledge the first and only time that the word inculturation has figured in a Roman Catholic ecclesiastical document of universal relevance was in the message to the people of God of the Synod of Bishops in 1977. There—at least, in Latin—the word inculturation is used in connection with catechesis, as ongoing evangelization.

The word was already used fifty years ago by a missiologist; he was using French and he built on the parallel of incarnation. "Incarnation is the word which the church has coined to express the mystery of the Word of God being made Flesh, expressing himself in human form, that is, incarnation." Similarly the Word of God, which is the message of salvation entering the human heart— of an individual or of a group—finds expression in the whole human way of life of that particular group or individual, and that is "inculturation." It is a kind of ongoing incarnation and that, I think, is the meaning given to it today.

In that connection, and already beginning to touch on *Evangelii Nuntiandi,* I propose some reflections about what exactly is meant by culture in this context. Pope Paul says very clearly that by culture we don't just mean art or a few manifestations of human genius; we mean simply the whole way of life of an individual and especially of a group, of a community—linguistic or ethnic. Everything that makes up the life of a people is their culture, and he refers to *Gaudium et Spes* in this context. So really it means human beings as they actually live out their lives. Now culture taken in its very broad and comprehensive sense has many functions in human life; I would like to pick out one that is of particular relevance to our problem. It is this: culture is the means through which persons develop in order to harness the resources of human nature. Just as technology harnesses the forces of nature so that they

Fr. Parmananda Divarkar is a Jesuit priest from India and a member of the General Superiors Council in Rome.

can serve human purposes and contribute to human progress, so culture harnesses the human resources of the human race and of the human individual and makes them available for the progress of the individual and for the progress of society as a whole.

There is here not a vicious circle but a virtuous circle, which we also find in technology. The progress of technology helps us to exploit the forces of nature. The more forces of nature we have available to us, the more technology progresses, and the progress of technology gets hold of other forces of nature and this goes on in a geometric progression of technology, as is happening today—almost too fast for us to cope with. In a very similar manner, but perhaps more slowly, the more resources are brought into operation, the further culture develops.

Pope Paul says culture does not necessarily mean refinement of the human genius. Any way of life that a people has managed to live with is their culture, however minimally developed it may be. The basic thing is survival; the first thing that any human being wants is survival. Culture is the means whereby human beings learn to cope with their environment and so develop and reach maturity.

Development, maturity, and so on, cannot be defined in human terms. We cannot define what maturity is just as we cannot define life: it is a basic concept, and maturity is intimately connected with life. It is the perfect development of life—there are no definitions—but maturity can be measured in terms of the ability to cope with the environment of one's surroundings. It may help to clarify ideas if one distinguishes three stages of the maturing process, three stages of the ability to cope with one's environment.

The first stage is minimal; one can cope to the extent of surviving. Survival as such is not maturity; for newborn infants the first thing is survival. The next stage is when you can cope with the environment to the extent of making use of it for your own purposes. Obviously these states are not completely separated one from another.

The third and final stage of maturity is when a living being can contribute to the environment, can create, procreate, and produce. That is real maturity for a living being: when you can propagate the race, keep it going, embellish, improve the environment. These are the three stages of the ability to cope, and they have very much to do with culture. The minimal culture enables us to survive; the development of culture enables us to utilize fire and so on; and eventually we are able to produce, to create through means of culture, and, in that way, to develop ourselves.

Culture is the means that we develop in order to be able to exploit our inner resources. Once we have developed them and learned to handle them, there is very little difference between the means to exploit resources and the resources themselves.

An example may help. Take electricity. I know if I put on the switch the light comes on, and I don't bother about how the electricity is produced and what would happen if there were no generators. I know nothing about that. It is the same with culture. We don't distinguish those inner resources, those generators that produce and make available the resources. We take our resources for granted because we have learned to handle the means to use those resources.

Now the problem that is facing us today, both in culture and in faith (and that is where we come to inculturation), is this: because of change, often those means that we once used are no longer adequate. This becomes a very big problem for the younger generation. The means that help us to exploit our inner resources are no longer adequate for the new generation, and this causes a so-called cultural crisis. The younger generation even look for a new language to be able to express themselves, express their new experiences. The way to cope with such a situation is to get into direct contact with those resources and not to be so dependent on cultural forms and channels of cultural expression which are no longer adequate.

There again examples help. I was in Rome at our renewal chapter, in 1965 and 1966, and again at the chapter in 1974 and 1975. One difference I saw was this: in 1965 (we were over two hundred there) we were still able to communicate in Latin, all could manage to understand and express ourselves in Latin. The result was that people who handled Latin well obviously had an advantage; the better you knew Latin, the better you could communicate. In 1974 that was no longer the case. Either people did not understand Latin or they did not want to admit that they knew Latin. The fact was, Latin was out. We had to manage with a lot of languages. In the second situation it was better to know a number of languages badly, than to know one language well. You could get across more using a variety of languages to a wider circle; if you tried to cultivate one language well you could be at a disadvantage.

That is the situation we are at with our culture now. Formerly, there was one culture for any given group and it was the means of communication for development. The more you developed it, the more you could get across and develop yourself. Today we are in a situation where no one given means is absolutely sure to "deliver the goods." What do we do? The main thing is to get hold of the resources; this is happening also with the faith. Our faith is also a resource given us by God, not a natural resource but a supernatural resource, and in the course of history we have found ways to express that faith. We have found satisfying expressions that have helped us to develop our faith, to strengthen our faith, to pass on our faith to our children. Today, that doesn't happen, and we feel there is a crisis of faith; but it's only a crisis of expression of faith. It's no use crying that we do not have an expression of faith; the main thing is to have faith, and to be able to get that across even if it is in a number of badly spoken languages.

Again Pope Paul reminds us: when we speak of languages, we don't just mean words of a vocabulary; we mean the whole method whereby human beings express themselves and communicate with one another. This is a point which seems to be fairly important to consider when we speak of the problem of inculturation: that somehow we must find means of expressing ourselves.

Pope Paul said that the rupture between the gospel message and culture is the drama of our days, as it has been in all ages.

Why is it so? Basically, it seems to be this: the Gospel is already wedded to one very particular culture, the culture in which Christ, Our Lord, was born, lived, and expressed himself. It already has a culture; so how do you wed it to another culture without divorcing it from the first culture? That is a basic problem and it came up immediately in the Acts of the Apostles, when the first disciples thought that in order to be a Christian, you had to be a Jew. The apostles, after discussing this, said: "No, you don't have to pass through the Mosaic Law." But it's pretty obvious from the history of the church that this statement did not really solve the problem. In fact the problem became more and more acute until the present situation when we are asking ourselves: what did they do about it? The reason is that the gospel, and therefore the spread of the gospel, is independent of any and every culture. They have their own culture to the extent that they have taken to heart their faith, to the extent that their faith is very much wedded to their culture. When they want to get that faith across to others, again what do they do? How do they disassociate, how do they abstract that faith? That is what Pope Paul is asking us to do.

But what is the essence of the faith? It's the way I commit myself to God. How do I get others to commit themselves to God, in their own way of expressing the commitment and love? There is obviously a problem there. How do I communicate faith to others without imposing on others my culture? I mean by culture even my mental framework, my terms of reference, my way of speaking. If we could answer that, then maybe we would find a way to solve the deeper and more fundamental problem of how and to what extent we can disassociate the so-called essence of the faith from the cultural context of the gospel.

When evangelizers, missionaries, messengers, establish dialogue with an individual or a group to whom they are coming with the Good News, the way the dialogue goes depends very much on who starts asking the questions. What has happened traditionally? We start asking questions: Why do you do this? Why do you not observe this? That is what the Jews did with the pagan Christians: they started asking the questions and put the other person on the defensive. You are at an advantage if you start the attack, so I suggest that you let the other one start asking the questions. "Why is it that you have come out here to tell me this?" "What does it mean in your life?" "Why have you connected this with something else?" That would make us think twice about what we are getting across, to make distinctions between the resources and the way we exploit these resources.

One other point which Pope Paul brings up, by implication, is that the spread of the gospel and of the church is not a territorial expansion; it is not a question of planting communities on a greater surface of the globe. It is a reaching out to peoples in different situations so that the faith and life of the church will be enriched because we find newer expressions. He is speaking of qualitative progress, not quantitative, as we were thinking of before. Spreading the same product all over the world is not the important thing; it is rather that different human situations are reaching and accepting the gospel, and expressing it in their own terms. He implies (but does not develop the point) that then we will have as many forms of Christianity as there are people in this world. Then what is going to happen? Where is the unity of the church? Some feel that there is far too much pluralism in the church since the Vatican Council: practically everyone doing his or her own thing, and if we start encouraging that, there will be total chaos. Many say there is a crisis of faith, and so there is. We find it among priests, committed Christians, religious, teenagers —no one knows what is right or wrong. There is some truth in that. One could make a good case and argue in the reverse, that for many of these people, the crisis is not in their faith, but because they can't find a satisfactory, meaningful expression of it. So the problem is insufficient pluralism. People's faith is in crisis because there is not sufficient pluralism for them to find expression of the faith that is really meaningful, in which they really feel committed to God in Christ.

I will conclude with one example. Language keeps changing all the time and today more than ever because there are new experiences that people try to express with new words. One of the problems of a family is that the children are talking a language different from their parents, and they really cannot understand each other. There is the Queen's English, American English, Indian English, and so on. When all is said and done we each have our own language. Yet I hope we can communicate. Even though a person may be speaking a different language, there are ways of getting across; human nature is basically the same.

I think eventually we will have to accept that, for the church and for the expression of our faith, which is our Christian life in the church, there will be something that is basically the same, and groups will have more things in common. But each one of us will have his or her own faith expression, his or her own way of living the Christian commitment, and there is nothing to worry about in that.

25

INCARNATING THE MESSAGE OF CHRIST IN DIFFERENT CULTURES

Walbert Bühlmann

A transnational person is a person accepted in any culture as if it were her or his own. Probably this would not be possible even for God Almighty, because it is a contradiction in itself. All that is individual is concrete; we get universal ideas only by abstraction. Christ was not a transcultural man; he was very much inculturated in his own culture—by his language, by his clothes, even by his religion. He was a man of his people. They say that the gospel from the beginning has never been published *in statu puro*. It has always been published incarnated in a concrete culture; even the four Gospels we have are not just four times the same thing, but each Gospel is a new process, a new state, a bigger incarnation of the same message of Christ. St. John incarnated his Gospel in the milieu of Greek philosophy. The same church was incarnated in the Judeao-Christian milieu, in the Greek milieu, Roman milieu, in the German-Celtic milieu, and so in the first millennium milieu. The church was very flexible, capable of being incarnated in the different cultures it met on its way.

But then came a static period. The church became static, and, especially since the discovery of the New World, the church began to export its own Western culture, its own Western form. It is strange that the Western form of being a Christian led to the belief that the Western form was the only legitimate form of being a Christian. This was a very wrong conclusion. The right conclusion would have been that, if it was possible to produce the Western form of being a Christian, then it should also be possible to produce the Eastern form, the African form, the Asian form, and the Latin American form of being Christian. But we know that for five centuries there was only one form of the Catholic church, the Western form, and we have had it since the Council of Trent. After the First Vatican Council we stressed uniformity very much: one church, one central power in the church—therefore uniformity in the church. But for the past twenty years, since the end of the Second

Fr. Walbert Bühlmann is a Swiss member of the Capuchin Order and a former missionary in Tanzania. At present he is Theology Mission Director for the Capuchins and is based in Rome.

World War, we know that step by step the world has become an emancipated world. There was an end of European hegemony: politically, economically, and culturally; now all the six continents have their own consciousness: political, cultural, economic. They also have an ecclesiastical consciousness.

In particular we have gotten new theological insights. The First Vatican Council laid stress on one church, one central power, infallibility and universal jurisdiction of the pope; the Second Vatican Council, completing the insights of the First Vatican Council, spoke of the local churches, and therefore, by necessity, of a legitimate pluriformity. In the conciliar texts this idea of legitimate pluriformity is expressed very prudently, very cautiously, because it was the very first time that the church officially spoke of pluriformity. Therefore it was obvious that we had only uniformity up till then.

Ten years after the Vatican Council, in *Evangelii Nuntiandi*, the same idea of pluriformity is expressed much more clearly, and not just as a right, as a postulate, but as a duty. For instance, *Evangelii Nuntiandi*, no. 63, a very strong text, says that the local churches have the duty, not only the right, but the duty, to incarnate the gospel message into the different languages, not only semantic languages, literal languages, but into the cultural languages, so that this message can be understood by those peoples. This translation has to be done in theological expression, catechetical expression, liturgical expression, and in the secondary church structures. In theological documents it is now very clear that the local churches have the right and the duty to incarnate the Gospel and the whole church life into their own culture.

That means local churches are not only a group of people in Africa or in Asia or anywhere, but they are a group of people in whom the gospel is incarnated. Local church is not only a geographical term meaning to be church in Africa or in Asia, but it is an essential ontological term meaning a group of people in whom the gospel is incarnated, in whom, therefore, new forms of church life are experienced and are approved. Theologically we are, therefore, at the end of a process of reflection, and we have attained an insight that corresponds to the new reality of this world. The practice is not yet so clear, and at this present time we are in a period of tension. The two powers in the church, the central power as in Vatican I and the episcopal power as in Vatican II, are two poles in the church. They have to be in equilibrium, but to get this equilibrium between the First and Second Vatican Councils we need a real dialogue.

The central power will always look for uniformity. The episcopal power will look for pluriformity. The two aspects are legitimately related, but they have to be balanced. Therefore the episcopal power—the local churches—have to get into a real dialogue; they have not only not to give in to the central idea, uniformity, but they have to fight for pluriformity. Not to fight against the church of Rome but to fight with the church of Rome, so that the new aspects of pluriformity, of incarnating the gospel in the different cultures, are really executed and implemented, not only in theory, but in practice.

In my traveling I have met many missionaries. One of them had a collection of sea shells; you can see how many hundreds of different forms of sea shells there are. Another one has a collection of butterflies—again you can see a tremendous number of forms of butterflies; another has a collection of orchids. If you look at creation, you see a richness in different colors and forms; the spirit of creation is so rich.

I cannot understand how the church, composed of human beings who are created according to the image of God and the spirit of creation, could be uniform.

In the field of liturgy I think we are happy to have gotten in the Second Vatican Council a new way of performing our liturgy; we are happy to have it in our own language, with some local expressions. If you travel in Africa, Asia, and Latin America you see how much the people there by their great spontaneity and creativity have developed new liturgies. I assisted one Sunday in a Zairean liturgy about a year ago in Kinshasa itself and in another diocese elsewhere in Zaire, and there you have a liturgy which goes on for two hours. The church is full of people, children, men, women, and this liturgy is really a celebration, a full participation of the whole people of God. It is a drama, and all the people are praying, singing, waving hands and bodies with processions, entrances, offertory. The text is concrete and understood by the people in their own context. I think such a liturgy is a happy experience for the people every Sunday.

During the week they have a hard life. They live in poverty, they have no work, they have troubles, problems, but on Sunday, they have an experience full of hope and of joy. You should hear the whole group of them sing, "Our Father in heaven, hallowed be thy name, thy kingdom come, thy will be done on earth as it is in heaven. Give us this day our daily bread in our small hands, forgive us our sins." It is a group of people like you see in a theater—a drama.

Now this is a very fine example of incarnation of the liturgy. But you see the tension of which I spoke. The liturgy in Zaire is not legal. They do it against the will of Rome. I read the correspondence Kinshasa had with Rome. The Episcopal Conference asked four years ago for approval of this Zaire liturgy. They sent the text, they sent the music on tapes, they sent photographs and slides on how they do it, and Rome allowed it only experimentally, which means in small groups and not in parish churches, without any publicity, for a certain time. Now this time—four years—is finished and the liturgy will be allowed no more. But yet they continue to do it publicly in many parish churches. They know they will not go back, and Rome knows that they do this liturgy. Rome is not happy with it, but they can no longer say: you are not allowed to do this. It is a typical case of tension between a local church—bishops and the people of God—and the Roman church: two different conceptions of being church. This is a case of a positive tension in the church for the good of the church.

There is a similar case in India. For several years there was an Indian liturgy. They had a Roman missal and Roman liturgy, but in some cases, especially in small groups, they had a complementary Indian liturgy composed by experts. Rome sent a letter to the Indian Bishops' Conference saying that the liturgy which had been tested for some years was no longer allowed.

At that time I spoke with some people in Rome. How is it possible that there is a real contradiction between the documents of Vatican II and *Evangelii Nuntiandi* and their concrete realization. As soon as a local church takes some concrete steps at being a local church, and not just a copy of the church of Rome, then Rome says in the name of the universal church, "You are not allowed to do this." As you know, about two hundred years ago we had the problem of the Chinese rites when a similar experiment was forbidden at the end of a long discussion. Today everybody agrees that the decision was a bad decision and that the church in Asia continued to remain a foreign element; it was not a church incarnated into the Asian culture. How can one repeat what is practically the same decision? As soon as an Indian or African church tries to become incarnated, in the name of the universal church, it is told: "Oh no, you are not allowed to do this." Many people, bishops and priests in Rome, say that the liturgy is the answer of the universal church to God. I think that this outlook is theologically wrong, liturgy is not the answer of the universal church. The universal church as such does not exist. What exists are thousands of local churches and they need a liturgical expression in their own languages, in their own symbols, in their own cultures, to respond to the one message of God. And these many local churches form the one universal church.

That is the tension. Experts in liturgy agree that after the council we had to take three steps. The first step was to get the renewed liturgy with commentaries, and this work has been well done.

The second step was to translate this renewed liturgy into the many languages—this has also been done.

The third step, they said, would be that of incarnating this renewed liturgy into the many cultures. This third step has not only not been done, but practically is no longer agreed to, no longer allowed, by the central power of the church—Rome. This is the tension in which we stand now. Theologically, it is clear; in practice we have to endure this tension. We have to fight for pluriformity, knowing that the unity of the church is not so much guaranteed by imposing a human uniformity, but is guaranteed by spiritual powers. Unity in the church is not uniformity, but is the one spirit, that one faith in Christ, one charity, love among each other, *koinonia*, exchanging pastoral experiences, and so on. These are the real elements of unity in the church—not mere external uniformity.

It is tragic that we have so much force and energy to expend for this purpose inside of the church, whereas we need so much force to be expended between the church and the world. How to bring our message to the world? This is the real problem of the church, and so it's all the more pitiful that we have to expend so much energy and time on our own internal problems.

We are at the beginning of a tremendous new era of theologizing. I would say we are at the beginning of the discovery of new theological space. We know that astronauts have taken tremendous steps, but that they are in fact very small steps. The astronauts will never come to the other end of outer space, and so I say we are also at the beginning of a new discovery of theological space. Up till now we have lived in an introverted theological world. We have had very clear responses formulated in catechisms, in theological proofs, and, thirty years ago when we studied theology, a manual of Tanqueray, or any other famous manual of the day, we could say: "Now I know theology." Most priests stopped studying theology saying, "I know it now—I have nothing more to learn." Today, however, and since we have discovered anew and looked behind those "proofs" and those dogmas, we have discovered tremendous "space openings." During the past twenty years we have seen a tremendous outburst of theologizing; so much so that it is impossible today to follow the full development. Karl Rahner said in an interview when he was seventy years old—five years ago: "When I began teaching theology I knew one-quarter part of it at that time, but now today I know perhaps one-fortieth part of it."

One phenomenon is especially interesting; namely, that in the past, only one continent was theologizing—our Western continent—and we practically repeated the one theology, that of Thomas Aquinas, in different editions, content that we had one universal theology even if a very abstract theology. Now we know that every continent has theological colleges, theological radio stations, and theologians. And more important than the official theologians in every continent, we have the basic communities who read the gospel together, who explain to each other the gospel, who are doing existential theology, and therefore in the future we will have a real spring of theologizing in all of the six continents. This theology will no longer be a universal theology. That means the light of the gospel, which is the same for all cultures and churches, casts a new light in different situations: what theologians today speak of as contextual theology. They ask how the one gospel can bring its light and force to this concrete context, to this concrete situation, so that people can live the gospel in the light of their situation and respond to this challenge to their situation.

Therefore today we need a "compared" theology. It is impossible to know all the theologies of the Third World, but nevertheless the best books and the best ideas should be exchanged. This is the new situation of the church. We are no longer a Western church, but are in contact with other churches and must exchange our theology with them and receive their theology into our own knowledge.

If we also apply this reflection to the field of moral theology, we will see that we are really at the very beginning of a new era of theologizing. We also exported our moral theology with the boast that it, and our own insights, were valid for all cultures. Today we see the very big problem this has caused, for instance, in Africa. They have trial marriages with polygamy, for example, which they can practice with a good conscience according to their customs. They practice a form of living in a family in marriage—the trial marriage in different steps—but we foreigners come and say, "Oh no, what you are doing is a mortal sin." So all these young Christians are excommunicated for several years from the sacraments because they follow their traditional way in marriage. The theologians were very well prepared. They did a study for two years with questionnaires. They knew the exact problem, the many difficulties there are regarding family and marriage. But in fact they could not decide on anything new. At the end of their meeting all they could say was, "We have to go on studying our problems."

In the past it was the task of the missionary institutes to bring the mission contacts, mission insights and experiences to our churches, to convince our priests and our church people that they had to give some money for the missions, and get some vocations for the missions. That was the monopoly of the missionary institutes. Since Vatican II we know that the church by nature is a missionary church. We have now not only the decree *Ad Gentes* but we have also *Lumen Gentium*, where the real missionary dynamic of the church entered all documents of the Vatican Council. Therefore today a priest or a theologian can no longer be said to be updated if he or she does not insist on the missionary nature of the church.

In our catechesis—for our children, our youngsters, our adult people—we must—all missionaries, priests, bishops, and laypeople—insist on the missionary nature of the church. In the past we were baptized in the church in order to save our souls; in the popular "missions" we preached about saving our souls. Today we say that for this salvation we do not really need to be baptized. We admit today, that even those outside the official church can save their souls. But to be baptized in the church means to be called to a greater witness; to bring the witness of the gospel to others; to be a sign for others who are not baptized. And so this new insight, that we as Christians have really a mission to others, to unknown church people not yet Christians, is the real meaning of being baptized.

In the mission countries and in the young churches, catechesis has this new aspect, namely, that today we have to start with the pre-Christian religions. In 1975 the Urban University of Propaganda Fide in Rome organized a missiological Congress on Evangelization and Cultures. In this context I took the topic "The New Theology of Non-Christian Theology and Catechesis," and for this purpose I wrote to eight higher institutes for catechetics, four in Africa and four in Asia. I asked two questions. Thirty years ago, in your country, did the catechisms you had speak of non-Christian religions—yes or no? Most of them said no. They simply began with our faith, with Christ, with the church, with the sacraments. They brought in a very new religion which had no relation with the old existing religions. If in some cases they spoke of these religions, they did so only in negative terms, condemning them as bad religions, as the work of the devil to be abandoned.

The second question I asked was this. Today, do the catechisms in your country speak of these religions? If yes, in what terms? And the responses now were quite different. All of them said, of course we speak of these religions, and we speak of them in positive terms. We start from the experience of our catechumens and then explain the meaning of their non-Christian religions, and how they have to be implemented and fulfilled in the message of Christ. To me therefore it is necessary that we start by bringing unity between the non-Christian religions and the Christian religion, to bring both into harmony so that God's plan of salvation is bigger than was supposed until now.

We are at the beginning of a new age, the coming of the third church. The pontificate of Paul VI was for me a turning point in church history. Before him we had a predominance of the Western church in all regards. In the fifteen years of Paul VI, Rome has become a world church—the center of gravity of Christianity has shifted from our Western world to the Southern world. From the beginning of our church history until a few years ago, the vast majority—85 percent of all Christians—were still living in the Western world of Europe and North America. Now this has already shifted, and as time goes on, the majority will be living in Latin America, Africa, and Asia. In twenty years, probably 70 percent of Catholics will be living in the southern hemisphere in each of these three continents.

Pope Paul VI also gave to these local communities their own bishops. In Africa, practically 75 percent of the bishops are indigenous; in Asia it is practically 100 percent. The same is true of the cardinals. Twenty years ago when John XXIII was elected, Africa did not have any cardinal; Asia had two. In the last two conclaves, Africa had twelve cardinals and Asia had the same. And again in retrospect: since the first pope, Peter, came to Rome, no pope came from outside Europe. Paul VI, by visiting all of the six continents, showed that the church officially is no longer a Western church, but a church of the six continents. And again in his pontificate, the Episcopal Synod of 1974 took place; for me it was a turning point in church history. One can still say that the Second Vatican Council and the three synods were made by Western bishops and Western theologians; the Fourth Synod of 1974 was clearly made by the theologians and bishops of the Third World. They prepared the important ideas which were taken up by *Evangelii Nuntiandi.* And we can foresee that the new inspiration and great ideas for the church will, in the future, come especially from the young churches of the Third World.

Culturally, however, with regard to the incarnation of the Gospel, we are really at the beginning of the Third Church, and I say the Third Church—not only the church of the Third World but at the same time the church of the third millennium. If we examine our church history we can see that the first millennium was under the leadership of the First Church, the Oriental church with Byzantium in the center, and the first eight councils were all held in the East. The second millennium was under the leadership of the Second Church, the Western church, our church, the church of missionary initiatives.

The coming third millennium will see the leadership of the Third Church, the Southern church. But we are only at the beginning of the third millennium, and the process of incarnation is merely a first step. In theology we see that the implementing of this incarnation will be the job of the next ten years, the next twenty years—the next millennium.